Mastering Forex Trading: Strategies for Success in the Global Currency Market

A Comprehensive Guide
to Unlocking Financial Freedom

Alexandra Thompson

Table of Contents

INTRODUCTION

Welcome to "Mastering Forex Trading: Strategies for Success in the Global Currency Market: A Comprehensive Guide to Unlocking Financial Freedom." In this comprehensive guide, we embark on a journey through the intricate world of Forex trading, offering you the essential knowledge, strategies, and mindset required to navigate this dynamic market successfully.

Forex trading, the largest global financial market, presents unparalleled opportunities for those seeking financial freedom. However, mastering Forex trading is not merely about predicting currency movements; it's about understanding the complexities of the market, managing risks effectively, and developing a disciplined approach to trading.

This book is designed to be your companion on this journey, whether you're a novice trader looking to build a solid foundation or an experienced trader aiming to refine your skills. We will start by demystifying the basics of Forex trading, including the history of the market, key participants, and fundamental concepts. From there, we'll delve into setting up your trading account, exploring essential tools and terminologies, and crafting a winning trading strategy tailored to your goals and risk tolerance.

Throughout this guide, you'll learn advanced technical and fundamental analysis techniques, risk management strategies, and the crucial role of trading psychology in achieving consistent success. With practical insights, real-world examples, and actionable advice, "Mastering Forex Trading" equips you with the knowledge and confidence to navigate the Forex market precisely and unlock your path to financial freedom.

CHAPTER I

Getting Started

Overview of the Forex Market

The forex market, or foreign exchange market, is the world's largest and most liquid financial market. It acts as a currency exchange platform for participants, including central banks, commercial banks, hedge funds, multinational organizations, and retail traders. The fundamental goal of the Forex market is to enable international trade and investment by allowing for the conversion of one currency into another.

Understanding currency pairs is a fundamental concept in the Forex market. Currencies are traded in pairs, with each pair representing the exchange rate between two currencies. The most commonly traded currency pairs, such as EUR/USD (Euro/US Dollar), USD/JPY (US Dollar/Japanese Yen), GBP/USD (British Pound/US Dollar), and USD/CHF, are categorized based on their liquidity and trading volume into major pairs, minor pairs, and exotic pairs.

One of the Forex market's distinguishing traits is its decentralized structure. Unlike traditional stock exchanges, which operate from specific physical locations, the Forex market is open 24 hours a day, five days a week, and across multiple time zones. This decentralized structure enables traders to engage in Forex trading anytime, providing enough possibilities for daily trading activity.

The interbank market, a crucial component of the Forex market, facilitates currency trading among major financial institutions. These institutions, including central banks, commercial banks, and investment banks, influence currency rates through their trading activities. Central banks, in particular, can intervene in the Forex market to support their local currencies or achieve specific monetary policy objectives.

The retail Forex market, a segment of the Forex market, is accessible to individual traders and investors. They can engage in Forex trading using online platforms provided by brokerage firms. The retail Forex market has witnessed significant growth in recent years, thanks to technological advancements and increased platform accessibility. Individual traders can now enter the Forex market with relatively small capital, enabling them to trade currencies from the comfort of their homes.

The Forex market is based on supply and demand, with currency values decided by buying and selling. Several factors influence currency rates, including economic indicators, geopolitical events, central bank policies, interest rates, and market sentiment. Traders use these indicators to predict future exchange rate movements and make informed trading decisions.

The Forex market provides traders with diverse trading opportunities, including spot trading, futures trading, options trading, and derivatives trading. Spot trading, the most prevalent type of Forex trading, is purchasing and selling currencies for immediate delivery at the current exchange rate. Futures trading is purchasing or selling currency contracts for future delivery at a preset price. Options trading gives traders the right, but not the responsibility, to buy or sell currencies at a specific price and time frame. Derivatives trading allows traders to bet on currency price swings without owning the underlying assets.

The Forex market is a dynamic and complicated marketplace in which currencies are traded around the clock, offering traders several possibilities to profit from exchange rate movements. Anyone interested in Forex trading should understand the market's fundamentals, such as currency pairs, trading hours, participants, and factors impacting exchange rates. With its decentralized structure, liquidity, and accessibility, the Forex market provides traders access to international finance and investment opportunities.

Importance of Forex Trading

Forex trading, or foreign currency trading, is fundamental in the global financial landscape for various reasons. At its foundation, forex trading is exchanging one currency for another, allowing businesses, governments, investors, and individuals to transact internationally. The significance of forex trading stems from its function as a facilitator of worldwide trade and investment. First, forex markets provide liquidity, allowing participants to purchase and sell currencies anytime, resulting in smooth transactions and price discovery. This liquidity is critical for enterprises involved in international trade because it will enable them to hedge currency risks and manage their exposure to exchange rate swings. Furthermore, forex trading helps maintain price stability by accurately representing various currencies' supply and demand dynamics, lowering volatility, and fostering economic stability.

Second, forex trading is critical in defining exchange rates, which determine the relative value of currencies and facilitate international trade and investment. Exchange rates impact the competitiveness of exports and imports, affecting business profitability and consumer purchasing power. As a result, governments and central banks closely monitor and occasionally intervene in currency markets to preserve stable exchange rates and achieve their economic goals. Furthermore, exchange rate fluctuations can affect investment returns and portfolio diversification methods, making forex trading an essential component of global investment markets.

Furthermore, forex trading promotes cross-border money flows and investment allocation, contributing to economic growth. Forex trading allows investors and speculators to profit from disparities in interest rates, inflation rates, and economic growth possibilities between countries. Forex markets enable efficient resource allocation by directing capital to where it is most productive, stimulating innovation, job creation, and economic development. Furthermore, forex trading promotes financial integration and globalization by connecting markets and participants worldwide, encouraging cross-border investment, trade, and cooperation.

In addition to its economic significance, forex trading provides numerous advantages to individual investors and traders. The currency market is open 24 hours a day, five days a week, giving participants flexibility and accessibility across time zones. Individuals can now trade currencies whenever they choose, allowing them to capitalize on market opportunities and effectively manage their financial portfolios. Furthermore, the forex market is very liquid and has low entry barriers, allowing even those with limited cash to participate in trading activities and potentially earn returns.

However, it is critical to note that forex trading carries dangers such as volatility, leverage, and geopolitical events, which can result in significant losses. Individuals who trade forex should educate themselves about the market, implement effective risk management procedures, and exhibit caution when trading currencies. Furthermore, regulatory monitoring and transparency are required to ensure the integrity and stability of currency markets, protect investors' interests, and maintain trust in the financial system.

Finally, forex trading is crucial because it facilitates worldwide commerce, investment, and economic development. Forex markets help to maintain global financial stability, growth, and integration by providing liquidity, establishing exchange rates, and facilitating capital flows. Furthermore, forex trading offers advantages to private investors and traders by increasing accessibility, flexibility, and possible profits. However, it is critical to understand the dangers connected with forex trading and implement innovative tactics to reduce them properly. Forex trading is essential to the current financial environment, propelling international transactions, investment flows, and economic growth.

Objectives of the Book

In the forex industry, books are invaluable resources that serve various purposes, from education and skill development to strategy creation and market analysis. Forex books teach beginners and prospective traders the fundamentals of currency trading, such as vocabulary, market dynamics, and trading strategies. These educational objectives are critical for beginners to learn the fundamentals of forex trading, understand the variables that influence currency fluctuations, and gain the skills to navigate the complex and dynamic forex markets. Furthermore, books frequently provide valuable insights into the psychology of trading, highlighting the significance of discipline, risk management, and emotional control in achieving long-term success as a forex trader.

Second, forex books are thorough guides for experienced traders looking to fine-tune their tactics, learn advanced trading techniques, and stay current on market events. These books cover topics like technical analysis, fundamental analysis, and market sentiment, providing in-depth analysis and practical insights to assist traders in improving their decision-making processes and trading performance. Furthermore, books on forex trading frequently include case studies, real-life examples, and practical exercises that allow traders to apply theoretical concepts to real-world trading circumstances, reinforcing their knowledge and expertise in forex trading.

Another goal of forex books is to give helpful tools for investors and portfolio managers who want to diversify their investments and properly manage currency risk. These publications provide insights into currency hedging strategies, portfolio optimization methodologies, and the significance of currencies in asset allocation, allowing investors to reduce currency risks while increasing risk-adjusted returns on their investment portfolios. Furthermore, forex trading books are geared toward professionals working in financial institutions, corporations, and government agencies, providing them with the knowledge and tools to make informed decisions about currency exposure, international transactions, and foreign exchange risk management.

Furthermore, forex books are essential in supporting innovation and thought leadership in the business by highlighting cutting-edge research, creative trading tactics, and developing currency market trends. Authors and specialists in the area frequently share their ideas, experiences, and viewpoints through books, contributing to the overall knowledge and understanding of forex trading among practitioners, academics, and enthusiasts. Furthermore, books serve as platforms for debate, discussion, and collaboration, allowing for the sharing of ideas and the development of novel ways to forex trading and market analysis.

To summarize, the purposes of forex books are multifaceted and diverse, including education, skill development, strategy design, market analysis, risk management, and innovation. Books, whether written for novices, seasoned traders, investors, or professionals, provide individuals with the knowledge, skills, and insights they need to thrive in the dynamic and competitive world of forex trading. Books help to grow, evolve, and progress the forex sector by giving comprehensive information, practical counsel, and thought-provoking viewpoints, allowing traders and investors to traverse the complexity of currency markets with confidence and competence.

CHAPTER II

Understanding the Basics of Forex Trading

What is Forex?

Forex, which stands for foreign exchange, is a decentralized worldwide marketplace where currencies are traded. It is the world's largest and most liquid financial market, with daily trading volumes over trillions of dollars. Forex trading is exchanging one currency for another at an agreed-upon price to profit from exchange rate swings. Unlike traditional stock markets, which are centralized and have fixed trading hours, the forex market is open 24 hours a day, five days a week, and spans multiple time zones worldwide. This continuous trading cycle ensures that forex participants, including central banks, financial institutions, corporations, governments, speculators, and individual traders, have access to liquidity and opportunities to trade currencies at all times, allowing for smooth transactions and price discovery.

The forex market is decentralized, with trading carried out electronically over the counter (OTC) via a network of interconnected banks, brokers, and financial institutions. This decentralization implies that no central exchange or regulatory entity regulates forex transactions, resulting in solid market transparency, accessibility, and competition. However, no centralized clearinghouse guarantees deal resolution or controls market conduct. Thus, participants must exercise prudence and due diligence when engaging in FX trading.

One of the distinguishing characteristics of the forex market is the trading of currency pairs, in which one currency is swapped for another. Each currency pair is quoted in terms of a base currency and a counter currency, with the exchange rate reflecting how much of the counter currency it takes to buy one unit of the base currency. For example, in the EUR/USD currency pair, the base currency is the euro (EUR), and the counter currency is the US dollar (USD). If the EUR/USD exchange rate is 1.20, one euro can be converted into 1.20 US dollars.

Forex trading provides a variety of ways for participants to profit from currency swings, such as speculation, hedging, arbitrage, and international trade. Speculators attempt to profit from short-term price swings by purchasing or selling currencies based on market expectations and analysis. Hedgers, such as multinational organizations and investors, employ forex derivatives, such as forward contracts and options, to reduce the risks associated with currency swings and protect their global business operations and investment portfolios. Arbitrageurs earn from risk-free trades by considering price differences between forex markets or currency pairings. At the same time, international businesses and travelers use forex services to expedite cross-border transactions and currency conversion.

However, it is critical to note that forex trading entails inherent risks such as market volatility, leverage, geopolitical events, and economic indicators, which can result in significant losses if not managed properly. As a result, forex market participants must be thoroughly aware of market dynamics, risk management techniques, and trading tactics and maintain discipline, patience, and emotional control. Furthermore, regulatory monitoring and transparency are critical to ensuring the integrity and stability of the currency market, protecting investors' interests, and sustaining trust in the financial system.

Finally, forex is a dynamic and decentralized marketplace in which currencies are traded 24 hours a day, seven days a week, allowing participants to profit from currency changes. Forex trading attracts a broad spectrum of participants, from individual retail traders to substantial financial institutions, due to its high liquidity, accessibility, and profit potential. However, participants must approach forex trading with caution, diligence, and education because it involves dangers and problems that must be carefully navigated and managed. Finally, forex continues to be a critical component of the global financial system, supporting vast international trade, investment, and economic growth.

History and Evolution of the Forex Market

The history and evolution of the forex market trace back centuries, evolving from rudimentary exchange systems to the dynamic and sophisticated market we know today. The origins of forex trading can be traced back to ancient times when merchants and traders engaged in barter transactions to exchange goods and services across different regions and civilizations. As commerce expanded and trade routes developed, the need for a standardized medium of exchange became apparent, leading to the emergence of currency as a means of facilitating trade.

One of the earliest forms of organized currency trading dates back to the Babylonian period, where merchants exchanged goods using silver and other precious metals as a medium of exchange. However, it wasn't until the Middle Ages that formalized currency exchange systems began to develop, with money changers and foreign exchange brokers facilitating transactions between different currencies and regions. These early exchange systems laid the groundwork for the modern forex market, providing the infrastructure and mechanisms for currency trading to thrive.

The forex market as we know it today began to take shape in the 19th century with the establishment of the gold standard, which pegged the value of currencies to a specific amount of gold. This system provided stability and credibility to global currencies, facilitating international trade and investment. However, the gold standard was eventually abandoned in the 20th century due to economic instability and the outbreak of World War I, leading to the emergence of fiat currencies and flexible exchange rates.

The post-World War II era marked a significant turning point in the evolution of the forex market with the establishment of the Bretton Woods Agreement in 1944. Under this agreement, major currencies were pegged to the US dollar, which was convertible to gold at a fixed exchange rate. This system provided stability to global currencies and facilitated the reconstruction of war-torn economies. However, the Bretton Woods system collapsed in the early 1970s due to mounting economic pressures and the inability of the US to maintain the convertibility of the dollar to gold.

Following the collapse of the Bretton Woods system, the forex market transitioned to a floating exchange rate system, where currency values were determined by market forces of supply and demand. This shift paved the way for the modern forex market, characterized by increased liquidity, volatility, and globalization. The advent of technology, telecommunications, and the internet further revolutionized the forex market, enabling real-time trading, electronic transactions, and global connectivity.

Today, the forex market operates 24 hours a day, five days a week, across different time zones, with trading volumes surpassing trillions of dollars daily. It encompasses a diverse range of participants, including central banks, financial institutions, corporations, governments, and individual traders. The market is driven by a multitude of factors, including economic indicators, geopolitical events, central bank policies, and investor sentiment.

In conclusion, the history and evolution of the forex market reflect the dynamic interpla The forex market has evolved over centuries from simple exchange systems to the dynamic and complex market we know today. Forex trading dates back to ancient times when merchants and traders used barter transactions to swap products and services between areas and civilizations. As commerce grew and trade routes extended, the necessity for a uniform medium of exchange became clear, resulting in the birth of currency to facilitate trade.

One of the earliest examples of organized currency trading may be traced back to the Babylonian period when merchants exchanged items for silver and other precious metals. However, in the Middle Ages, structured currency exchange systems emerged, with money changers and foreign exchange brokers enabling transactions between currencies and regions. These early exchange systems established the groundwork for today's forex market, providing the infrastructure and processes that allow currency trading to prosper.

The forex market as we know it began to emerge in the nineteenth century with the implementation of the gold standard, which tied the value of currencies to a set amount of gold. This arrangement gave global currencies stability and credibility, boosting international trade and investment. However, the gold standard was finally abandoned in the twentieth century due to economic instability and the advent of World War I, resulting in the rise of fiat currencies and variable exchange rates.

The Bretton Woods Agreement, signed in 1944, constituted a watershed moment in the history of the currency market. This arrangement tied significant currencies to the US dollar, which was convertible to gold at a predetermined exchange rate. This method stabilized worldwide currencies and aided in the recovery of war-torn economies. However, the Bretton Woods system disintegrated in the early 1970s due to mounting economic pressures and the United States' inability to convert the dollar to gold.

Following the fall of the Bretton Woods system, the forex market adopted a floating exchange rate system in which market forces of supply and demand set currency values. This transition laid the groundwork for the modern forex market, distinguished by increasing liquidity, volatility, and globalization. The introduction of technology, telecommunications, and the internet further transformed the forex market, allowing for real-time trading, electronic transactions, and global connectivity.

Today, the forex market runs 24 hours a day, five days a week, across many time zones, with trading volumes exceeding trillions of dollars daily. It includes a broad spectrum of participants, including central banks, financial institutions, enterprises, governments, and private traders. Various factors influence market performance, including economic indicators, geopolitical developments, central bank policy, and investor emotion.

Finally, the history and growth of the forex market demonstrate the dynamic interplay of economic, political, and technological forces that shape global trade and finance. From its early beginnings as a barter system to its current incarnation as a vast and liquid market, forex trading has promoted international trade, investment, and economic progress. As the FX market evolves and adapts to changing circumstances, its importance and impact on the global economy will likely remain paramount for many years. Y of economic, political, and technological forces shaping global commerce and finance. From its humble origins as a barter system to its modern incarnation as a vast and liquid market, forex trading has played a pivotal role in facilitating international trade, investment, and economic development. As the forex market continues to evolve and adapt to changing realities, its significance and impact on the global economy are likely to remain paramount for years to come.

Key Participants in Forex Trading

The forex market is a dynamic and decentralized marketplace where currencies are traded, and its operation is strongly dependent on the participation of numerous significant participants. Central banks participate in forex trading, shaping exchange rates, and implementing monetary policy. Central banks, such as the Federal Reserve in the United States, the European Central Bank, and the Bank of Japan, intervene in forex markets to stable their currencies, regulate inflation, and promote economic growth. Central banks control currency supply and demand through open market operations, interest rate adjustments, and foreign exchange interventions, which affect exchange rates and market sentiment.

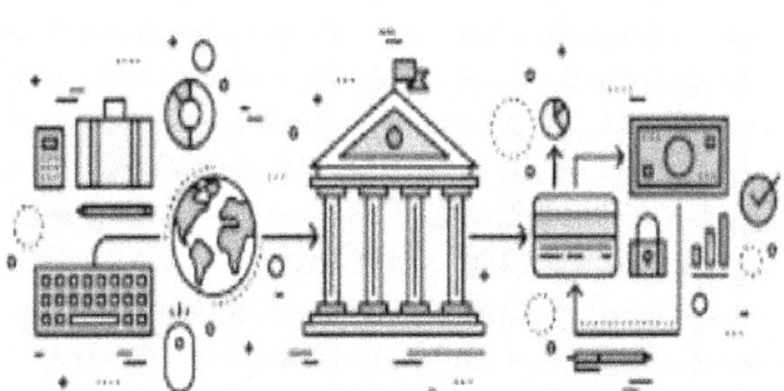

Commercial banks also play an important role in forex trading, acting as mediators between clients and counterparties. These banks add liquidity to the market by quoting bid and ask prices for currency pairings and carrying out trades on behalf of their clients, which include multinational corporations, institutional investors, and retail traders. Commercial banks also engage in proprietary trading, speculating on currency movements to make profits and control exposure to currency risks. Furthermore, significant banks participate in the interbank market, which allows financial institutions to trade huge volumes of currency at wholesale rates.

Institutional investors, such as hedge funds, pension funds, and asset managers, are essential participants in forex trading. They allocate capital to currency markets as part of their investment plans. Institutional investors use forex trading to diversify their portfolios, hedge against currency risks, and capitalize on market trends. These investors often use sophisticated trading tactics such as trend following, carry trading, and algorithmic trading to reach their investing goals. Institutional investors help to improve market liquidity and efficiency because their trading activity accounts for a significant share of daily currency turnover.

Multinational firms play an essential role in forex trading because they use currency transactions to ease international trade and manage their exposure to foreign exchange risks. These businesses exchange currencies to pay for imports, repatriate earnings, and hedge against adverse currency swings that may affect their revenues and expenses. Furthermore, international firms may participate in speculative forex trading to benefit from favorable exchange rate changes and improve their financial performance. The magnitude and frequency of currency transactions by multinational firms help to increase the liquidity and depth of the forex market.

Retail traders are another critical group of forex traders, consisting of individual investors and traders who trade currencies for profit or speculation. With the introduction of Internet trading platforms and technical improvements, retail traders now have unparalleled access to the forex market. They can execute trades from anywhere globally using a computer or mobile device. Retail traders deal less than institutional participants but contribute significantly to market liquidity and volatility. Retail traders use a variety of trading tactics, including day trading, swing trading, and scalping, and frequently use leverage to maximize their potential earnings.

To summarize, the forex market is driven by the participation of several significant actors, including central banks, commercial banks, institutional investors, multinational corporations, and retail traders. Each participant contributes distinct motivations, ambitions, and trading tactics to the market, defining its dynamics and impacting exchange rates. The interaction and interplay of these participants help to maintain the forex market's liquidity, efficiency, and resilience, making it one of the most lively and accessible financial markets in the world.

Major Currency Pairs

In the enormous terrain of the forex market, specific currency pairings are the most widely traded and influential, referred to as major currencies. These pairs include the world's most liquid and heavily traded currencies, indicating the economies' strength, stability, and significance. The US dollar (USD) is usually matched with other major currencies, including the euro (EUR), Japanese yen (JPY), British pound (GBP), Swiss franc (CHF), Canadian dollar (CAD), and Australian dollar (AUD). These currency pairings have high trading volumes, tight bid-ask spreads, and significant market depth, appealing to traders and investors looking for liquidity and volatility.

One of the most popular main currency pairs is EUR/USD, which compares the euro to the US dollar. This pair accounts for a large amount of daily forex trading volume and is influenced by economic data, monetary policy choices, and geopolitical developments in the Eurozone and the United States. The EUR/USD pair is well-known for its tight spreads and high liquidity, making it a popular choice among traders looking for profit opportunities.

Another significant currency pair is USD/JPY, which compares the US dollar to the Japanese yen. Global financial markets' risk sentiment, interest rate differentials, and economic indicators all significantly impact the USD/JPY pair. Japan is a substantial exporter with a large current account surplus. In contrast, the US is a global economic superpower, making this pair especially vulnerable to fluctuations in trade flows and investor sentiment.

The GBP/USD pair, often called cable, pits the British pound against the US dollar. Economic data releases, monetary policy decisions by the Bank of England and the Federal Reserve, and political happenings in the United Kingdom, such as Brexit negotiations, influence this pair. The GBP/USD pair is noted for its volatility, with significant price movements in response to news events and market sentiments.

The USD/CHF currency pair, sometimes known as the "Swissie," pairs the US dollar with the Swiss franc. Switzerland is known for its stable economy, strong financial sector, and safe-haven status. Therefore, the USD/CHF pair is attractive during market volatility and risk aversion. This pair is affected by interest rate differentials, geopolitical tensions, and global economic conditions.

The USD/CAD pair exchanges the US dollar for the Canadian dollar, popularly known as the "loonie." Canada is a significant oil exporter, and the Canadian dollar is highly associated with oil prices. As a result, oil prices, economic data releases, and monetary policy choices made by the Bank of Canada and the Federal Reserve all impact the USD/CAD pair.

Finally, the AUD/USD pair pairs Australian and US dollars. Australia is a large supplier of commodities, particularly iron ore and coal, and the Australian dollar's value is tightly linked to commodity prices and global economic conditions. Chinese economic statistics, interest rate differentials, and financial market risk sentiment all impact the AUD/USD exchange rate.

To summarize, big currency pairs are the most actively traded and prominent in the forex market, representing the currencies of the world's major economies. These pairs provide strong liquidity, tight spreads, and significant market depth, making them appealing to traders and investors looking for opportunities in the currency markets. Each central currency pair has distinct characteristics, drivers, and variables impacting price movements, creating numerous chances for profit and risk management in the volatile world of forex trading.

Factors Influencing Exchange Rates

Exchange rates, which measure the value of one currency in comparison to another, are impacted by various factors that reflect the complex interaction of economic, political, and psychological forces in the global market. Interest rate differentials between countries are a fundamental factor in currency rates. Central banks alter interest rates to keep inflation under control, boost economic growth, and ensure financial stability. Higher interest rates encourage foreign investment, which increases the native currency, but lower interest rates negatively impact the currency.

Economic indicators and data releases also substantially influence currency rates. Key indicators such as GDP, inflation, employment, and trade balances shed light on an economy's health and performance. Positive economic data releases, such as strong GDP growth or falling unemployment rates, can boost currency confidence and lead to appreciation, while negative data releases can have the reverse impact, resulting in devaluation.

Political stability and geopolitical developments can affect currency rates by influencing investor confidence and risk sentiment. Countries with stable political environments and robust institutions attract foreign investment, which boosts their currencies. Political turbulence, social unrest, and geopolitical tensions, on the other hand, can cause capital flight and currency depreciation. Uncertainty over elections, trade talks, or diplomatic confrontations, for example, can induce changes in exchange rates as investors reassess risk.

Central bank actions and monetary policy decisions both impact exchange rates. Central banks may interfere in currency markets to stabilize exchange rates, prevent excessive volatility, or achieve specific policy objectives. For example, they may intervene in foreign exchange markets to weaken an overvalued currency to boost export competitiveness or to strengthen a falling currency to battle inflationary pressures.

Market mood and investor expectations are essential in setting exchange rates, typically driving short-term swings in currency markets—economic news, geopolitical happenings, central bank communications, and market speculation all impact sentiment. Positive mood can drive up demand for a currency, resulting in appreciation, while negative feelings can lead to selling pressure and depreciation.

Trade and capital flows impact exchange rates by influencing currency supply and demand. Trade flows are the transfers of products and services between countries, whereas capital flows are the movements of financial assets and investments. Countries with trade surpluses, or those that export more than they import, typically see their currencies appreciate, whereas countries with trade deficits may see their currencies depreciate. Similarly, interest rate differentials, economic growth predictions, and risk appetite can all influence capital flows and currency rates.

Finally, market speculation and intervention by market participants such as hedge funds, institutional investors, and individual traders can increase exchange rate volatility. Speculative trading activity, such as carry trades, trend following, and algorithmic trading, can increase short-term currency volatility, especially in highly liquid and accessible markets like forex.

Finally, exchange rates are impacted by a complex interaction of economic, political, and psychological variables. Understanding these elements and their repercussions is critical for traders, investors, governments, and enterprises attempting to navigate the volatile and interrelated world of currency markets. While short-term factors like news events and market emotion can impact exchange rates, long-term patterns are often driven by underlying economic fundamentals and structural factors that shape the global economy.

CHAPTER III

Setting Up Your Forex Trading Account

Choosing a Reliable Broker

Making choices with a reputable broker is critical for success in the forex market, as the broker acts as an intermediary between traders and the broad and volatile currency market. Choosing the proper broker can be difficult because so many brokers offer a wide range of trading services, platforms, and features. However, there are some essential things to examine while selecting brokers to verify their dependability, security, and suitability for your trading requirements.

First and foremost, regulatory compliance is essential when selecting a broker. Reputable brokers are licensed and regulated by recognized financial authorities in their jurisdictions, ensuring they follow stringent regulatory requirements and norms. Regulatory monitoring protects traders from fraud, manipulation, and unfair trading practices and provides avenues for dispute resolution. Before creating an account with a broker, you should check their regulatory status and ensure they can provide brokerage services in your country or region.

Another essential thing to examine is the broker's reputation and track record in the business. Trusted brokers often have a long track record in the industry and a strong reputation based on openness, integrity, and client satisfaction. Conducting extensive research, reading reviews, and obtaining recommendations from other traders can provide helpful information about a broker's dependability, professionalism, and service quality. Checking the broker's regulatory compliance history, previous disciplinary proceedings, and client feedback can also help determine their integrity and credibility.

Furthermore, assessing the broker's trading platform and technological infrastructure is critical. A reputable broker should provide a solid and user-friendly trading platform that includes real-time market data, powerful charting tools, and a variety of order types and execution options. The trading platform should work with various devices and operating systems, allowing traders to effortlessly access their accounts and execute transactions from PCs, laptops, cellphones, and tablets. Furthermore, the broker should invest in solid security measures, including encryption protocols, firewalls, and secure socket layer (SSL) technology to protect clients' personal and financial data from cyber threats and unauthorized access.

Transaction expenses and trading fees are also crucial when selecting a broker. While low spreads and charges can help decrease trading expenses and increase profits, it's essential to assess the broker's whole value offering, which includes execution quality, order filling speed, and customer service. Some brokers may provide commission-free trading but compensate by increasing spreads or charging hidden fees. So, traders should consider the pricing structure and trading terms carefully to ensure transparency and fairness.

Customer support and service quality are also important considerations that can significantly impact the trade experience. A credible broker should provide responsive and knowledgeable client service over various channels, including phone, email, live chat, and social media. Traders should promptly evaluate the broker's timeliness, professionalism, and ability to answer inquiries, technical challenges, and account-related matters. Furthermore, the broker's instructional resources, market research, and trading tools can increase traders' abilities, knowledge, and performance in the forex market.

Finally, you should assess the broker's reputation for order execution and trading transparency. A reputable broker should offer fair and transparent order execution without slippage, requotes, or manipulation. Traders should assess the broker's order execution speed, latency, and fill rates to ensure optimal trading conditions and reduce the risk of adverse market movements. Brokers should also disclose information about their liquidity providers, trading partners, and execution venues to ensure transparency and responsibility for their clients.

Selecting a reputable broker is an important decision that can considerably impact the success and profitability of your forex trading operations. Traders can make informed selections and choose a broker that best suits their needs and preferences by considering aspects like regulatory compliance, reputation, technology infrastructure, trading fees, customer service, and order execution quality. While selecting a broker may take some time and effort, the long-term benefits of trading with a reputed and trustworthy broker outweigh the investment.

Types of Forex Trading Accounts

Forex trading accounts are available in various categories, each tailored to meet the unique needs, preferences, and trading styles of individual traders. Understanding the many types of forex trading accounts is vital for determining the best option based on account size, leverage, trading platform, and trading circumstances.

The basic account is one of the most prevalent forms of forex trading accounts, and it is appropriate for beginners and intermediate traders. Standard accounts usually need a minimum deposit and provide access to many currency pairs, competitive spreads, and leverage options. Standard accounts allow traders to execute trades in standard lot sizes, with each lot representing 100,000 units of the base currency. Standard accounts offer flexibility and liquidity, making them perfect for traders seeking a balanced forex trading strategy with minimal risk exposure.

Another forex trading account is the mini account, designed for traders with limited funds or who choose to trade at lower risk levels. Mini accounts have a lower minimum deposit than regular accounts, enabling traders to execute trades in smaller lot sizes, often 0.1 lot or 10,000 units of the base currency. Mini accounts provide identical trading circumstances as regular accounts, including competitive spreads and leverage options, but with lower capital requirements and risk exposure. Mini accounts are popular with new traders who wish to get forex trading experience without investing vast amounts of money upfront.

Micro accounts are another forex trading account meant for traders with small trading money or desire to trade with low risk. Micro accounts have an even lower minimum deposit than mini accounts, allowing traders to make trades in micro lot sizes, typically 0.01 lot or 1,000 units of the base currency. Micro accounts allow traders to test their trading techniques, perfect their skills, and gain confidence in the forex market while incurring minimal financial risk. Micro accounts may have slightly greater spreads and lower leverage than standard and mini accounts, but they offer an affordable entry point for ambitious traders with minimal assets.

Managed accounts, often PAMM accounts, are available to traders looking for more leverage and possible rewards. Expert traders or money managers professionally manage accounts who trade for clients in exchange for a performance fee or profit-sharing agreement. PAMM accounts, which stand for the Percentage Allocation Management Module, enable investors to allocate assets to various managed accounts while sharing in the gains earned by money managers' trading operations. Managed accounts and PAMM accounts provide diversity, knowledge, and the possibility for higher profits, but they also carry more risk and may have a minimum investment requirement.

Additionally, some brokers provide specialty forex trading accounts, such as Islamic or demo accounts, to meet specific trading preferences or criteria. Islamic accounts, also known as swap-free accounts, adhere to Islamic Shariah law principles by not paying interest on overnight positions, making them ideal for Muslim traders who want to follow religious requirements. Brokers offer demo accounts, which allow traders to imitate real-time trading situations and test trading techniques without risking real money. Demo accounts are valuable tools for novices to learn the fundamentals of forex trading and practice their skills in a risk-free environment before moving on to live trading.

Finally, numerous forex trading accounts are designed to meet individual traders' diverse demands, preferences, and trading styles. Whether you're a newbie with low funds, an experienced trader looking for more leverage, or an investor seeking expert management, there's a forex trading account type for you. Understanding the features, benefits, and restrictions of various types of forex trading accounts allows traders to make informed decisions and choose the best option for achieving their forex trading goals.

Account Management and Security

For forex traders, account management and security are critical factors to consider because they secure trading cash and assets, as well as financial and personal information. Effective account management requires implementing strong security measures, following best practices, and keeping a close eye on account activity to reduce risks and guard against fraudulent or unauthorized access.

Selecting a reliable and trustworthy broker is one of the most essential parts of account management and security. Reputable brokers follow stringent regulatory requirements and client protection and security guidelines because they are licensed and governed by established financial authorities. Before opening an account, traders should make sure that their funds are held in segregated accounts and protected against insolvency or bankruptcy by doing extensive research, reading reviews, and confirming the regulatory status of brokers.

Traders should also use robust password security procedures to guard against unwanted access to their trading accounts. This entails creating distinct, complicated passwords for every trading account, changing them regularly, and, when practical, turning on two-factor authentication (2FA). By asking traders to provide a secondary verification code—such as a text message or authentication app—in addition to their password when accessing their accounts, two-factor authentication offers extra protection.

Additionally, as public Wi-Fi networks and shared devices are susceptible to hacking and spying, traders should use caution when accessing their accounts from these locations. To prevent sensitive information from being intercepted or accessed by unauthorized parties, safe and encrypted internet connections, such as virtual private networks (VPNs), must be used when accessing trading accounts from distant or unknown areas.

Additionally, traders should routinely check their accounts for any unauthorized transactions or suspicious activity and notify their broker immediately if they see any anomalies or irregularities. This entails regularly checking trade confirmations, transaction histories, and account statements to guarantee correctness and quickly identify illegal or fraudulent activity. It is recommended that traders maintain current contact details with their broker to get timely warnings and alerts regarding account activity and security-related matters.

Traders should be aware of internal risks, including emotional trading, excessive leverage, and inadequate risk management, in addition to safeguarding their trading accounts against external dangers. Emotions like impulsivity, fear, and greed can impair judgment and cause traders to make illogical judgments that cost them a lot of money. A disciplined and methodical attitude to trading, adherence to pre-established trading plans and risk management techniques, and refraining from trading with money they cannot afford to lose are all recommended for traders.

Additionally, to lower the risk of concentration and minimize possible losses from unfavorable market moves, traders should diversify their trading money among various currency pairings and assets. This involves reasonable capital allocation based on correlation analysis, risk-reward ratios, and market circumstances to maximize portfolio performance and reduce exposure to particular risks or events.

To sum up, account management and security are essential components of forex trading that call for careful attention to detail, alertness, and adherence to industry best practices to safeguard trade funds and assets, as well as financial and personal data, against loss, fraud, and unauthorized access. Within the dynamic and competitive forex market, traders can improve their overall security and peace of mind by selecting trustworthy brokers, putting strong password protection measures in place, keeping an eye on account activity, and managing risk sensibly.

Introduction to Trading Platforms

Trading platforms are a portal to the dynamic world of forex trading, giving traders access to real-time market data, charting tools, order execution capabilities, and analytical resources. These platforms are crucial tools for traders of all levels, from novices to experienced experts, because they make it easier to execute trades, analyze market patterns, and manage trading accounts. Understanding the features, functionalities, and types of trading platforms is critical for traders to choose the best solution that meets their trading objectives, preferences, and technical requirements.

One of the most frequent trading platforms is the desktop platform, installed on a trader's computer and accessed through a desktop application. Desktop systems include potent features and complex functionality, such as customizable charts, technical indicators, trading tools, and quick and dependable order execution. These platforms are perfect for traders who need full trading capabilities and want to trade from a dedicated workstation with a reliable internet connection.

MetaTrader 4 (MT4) and MetaTrader 5 (MT5) are popular desktop trading platforms used by traders worldwide because of their user-friendly interfaces, extensive charting features, and automated trading strategy support.

Another trading platform is a web-based platform, which may be accessed via a web browser without downloading or installing software. Web-based platforms are convenient and flexible, allowing traders to access their accounts and conduct trades from any internet-enabled device, such as desktops, laptops, cellphones, and tablets. These platforms often have a streamlined interface, essential charting tools, and basic trading functionality, making them ideal for traders who value accessibility and ease of use. Web-based platforms are also popular among traders who travel frequently or prefer to trade on the go rather than being bound to a specific device.

Mobile trading platforms are another platform created exclusively for smartphones and tablets, allowing traders to access their accounts and trade currencies from any location with an internet connection. Mobile platforms provide features and functionality similar to desktop and web-based systems, including real-time quotations, charting tools, and order execution capabilities, but with smaller screens and touch-based navigation. Mobile platforms allow traders to monitor markets, execute trades, and manage positions while on the go, making them perfect for busy traders who need access to the forex market at all hours. MetaTrader Mobile, cTrader Mobile, and Thinkorswim Mobile are among the most popular mobile trading systems.

When deciding on the best trading platform, traders should evaluate the type of platform and its features and functionalities. Real-time market data, configurable charts, technical indicators, and drawing tools for conducting technical analysis are all must-have features in a trading platform. Order types and execution capabilities are other important considerations, as traders need quick and dependable order execution to capitalize on market opportunities and adequately manage risk. Furthermore, support for automated trading tactics, such as expert advisors (EAs) and algorithmic trading, can help traders avoid emotional bias by automating their trading decisions.

Security and dependability are also crucial considerations when considering trading platforms, as traders must trust that their personal and financial information is safe from unauthorized access or cyber-attacks. Reputable brokers often provide trading platforms that use industry-standard security mechanisms like encryption, firewalls, and multi-factor authentication to protect client data and transactions. Furthermore, traders should evaluate the platform's uptime, stability, and performance to ensure a smooth trading experience without downtime or technical issues that could disrupt trading activities.

To summarize, trading platforms are critical tools for traders who want to enter the forex market, assess market trends, make transactions, and successfully manage their accounts. Understanding the many types, features, and functionalities of trading platforms allows traders to choose the best alternative for their trading goals, preferences, and technical requirements. Whether you prefer a desktop-based platform for complete trading capabilities, a web-based platform for convenience and accessibility, or a mobile platform for trading on the go, there is a trading platform to meet the demands of every trader in the dynamic and competitive forex market.

CHAPTER IV

Essential Tools and Terminologies

Candlestick Patterns

Candlestick patterns are crucial for forex traders, providing vital insights into the market mood, price dynamics, and future price reversals or continuations. These patterns are created by arranging candlesticks on price charts, each reflecting a specific trading period's open, high, low, and closing values, such as a minute, hour, day, or week. Candlestick patterns are divided into bullish and bearish patterns based on their implications for price movement. Bullish candlestick patterns signal potential bullish reversals or continuations, while bearish candlestick patterns signal potential bearish reversals or continuations.

The hammer is a well-known bullish candlestick pattern with a small body, a long lower shadow, and little to no upper shadow. Hammers are generally seen at the bottom of downtrends and signify potential bullish reversals when buyers move in to push prices higher following a period of selling pressure. Similarly, the inverted hammer is a bullish candlestick pattern distinguished by a small body, a long upper shadow, and little or no lower shadow. Inverted hammers emerge at the bottom of downtrends, indicating potential bullish reversals as buyers outnumber sellers and drive prices higher.

Bearish candlestick patterns, on the other hand, signal that the price may reverse or continue downward. One of the most common bearish patterns is the shooting star, which has a small body, a lengthy upper shadow, and little to no bottom shadow. Shooting stars usually appear at the top of uptrends, indicating probable negative reversals as sellers outnumber purchasers and force prices down. The bearish engulfing pattern happens when a substantial bearish candlestick engulfs the previous bullish candlestick, signaling that momentum has shifted from bullish to bearish.

In addition to individual candlestick patterns, traders look at combinations of candlesticks known as candlestick patterns. These patterns comprise two or more candlesticks that form distinctive shapes or formations on price charts, providing deeper insights into market dynamics and probable price moves. One of the most common candlestick patterns is the bullish engulfing pattern, which consists of a small bearish candlestick followed by a more significant bullish candlestick that engulfs the preceding candlestick's body. Bullish engulfing patterns indicate probable bullish reversals, in which buyers outnumber sellers and drive prices higher following a period of selling pressure.

Similarly, the bearish engulfing pattern consists of a small bullish candlestick and a larger bearish candlestick that engulfs the previous candlestick's body. Bearish engulfing patterns indicate probable bearish reversals, in which sellers outnumber buyers and drive prices lower following a period of buying pressure. Other popular candlestick patterns include doji, evening star, morning star, harami, and spinning top, each having its distinct qualities and consequences for price movement.

While candlestick patterns can provide valuable insights into market dynamics and potential price movements, traders must use them with other technical indicators, such as trend lines, moving averages, and support and resistance levels, to confirm signals and make sound trading decisions. Furthermore, traders should analyze the timescale and context in which candlestick patterns emerge, as patterns can have varying interpretations and implications based on market conditions and trading goals.

Finally, candlestick patterns are helpful for forex traders to monitor market mood, identify prospective reversals or continuations, and make sound trading decisions. Understanding the qualities and ramifications of bullish and bearish candlestick patterns can help traders improve their technical analysis skills and their ability to anticipate and respond to changes in market dynamics. To validate signals and reduce the risk of false signals, traders must employ candlestick patterns in conjunction with other technical indicators and take into account the timeframe and context in which patterns occur. With expertise and experience, traders may use candlestick patterns to gain an advantage in the volatile and competitive forex market.

Technical Indicators

Technical indicators are crucial for forex traders to monitor price patterns, discover prospective trade opportunities, and make sound trading decisions. These indicators are mathematical computations applied to historical price data that provide information about market dynamics, momentum, volatility, and prospective reversals or continuations. While several technical indicators are available, each with distinct qualities and applications, some of the most commonly used indicators are moving averages, oscillators, and trend-following indicators.

Moving averages are among the most basic and widely utilized technical indicators in forex trading. These indicators smooth out price volatility and show the underlying trend direction by average closing prices over a set number of periods, such as 10, 20, or 50. Simple moving averages (SMAs) offer equal weight to all price points in the calculation. In contrast, exponential moving averages (EMAs) give greater weight to recent prices, making them more sensitive to short-term fluctuations. Moving averages can determine trend direction, support and resistance levels, and potential entry and exit opportunities based on price crossovers and interactions with moving average lines.

Another type of technical indicator is oscillators, which indicate overbought or oversold market circumstances and prospective trend reversals. These indicators bounce between specified upper and lower limits, with readings above the higher boundary indicating overbought conditions and readings below the lower border indicating oversold conditions. Popular oscillators include the relative strength index (RSI), stochastic oscillator, and commodity channel index (CCI), providing information on market momentum, strength, and potential turning points. Traders utilize oscillators to confirm trend signals, detect price and oscillator divergence, and generate buy or sell signals based on overbought or oversold circumstances.

Trend-following indicators are technical tools that help to detect and confirm the direction of price trends while filtering out noise and market variations. These indicators are intended to capture the momentum of price changes and provide alerts for entering or exiting trades in the current trend's direction. Moving average convergence divergence (MACD), average directional index (ADX), and parabolic SAR (stop and reverse) are three popular trend-following indicators. Traders utilize trend-following indicators to identify trend reversals, quantify trend strength, and maintain alignment with the dominant market direction for the best trading results.

In addition to these broad categories of technical indicators, specialist indicators concentrate on specific aspects of price behavior, such as volume, volatility, and market mood. Volume indicators, such as on-balance volume (OBV) and volume-weighted average price (VWAP), quantify trading activity and shed light on the strength and longevity of price trends. Volatility indicators, such as Bollinger Bands and Average True Range (ATR), quantify market changes and assist traders in identifying probable price movements and establishing optimal stop-loss and take-profit levels. Mood indicators, such as the put/call ratio and the commitment of traders (COT) report, provide information on market mood and positioning among traders and institutions, allowing traders to measure sentiment and forecast probable price reversals or continuations.

While technical indicators can provide valuable insights into market dynamics and potential trade setups, traders must use them cautiously and in conjunction with other types of analysis, such as fundamental and market sentiment analysis, to validate signals and make sound trading decisions. Furthermore, traders should be aware of the limitations and disadvantages of technical indicators, such as lagging indications, misleading signals, and susceptibility to market conditions, and adjust their trading methods accordingly. With practice, expertise, and a strong understanding of technical indicators, traders can use these tools to acquire a competitive advantage in the volatile and competitive forex market.

Fundamental Analysis

Fundamental analysis is critical to forex trading, providing traders with significant insights into currencies' intrinsic value, economic fundamentals, and market patterns. Unlike technical analysis, which focuses on past price data and market activity, fundamental analysis investigates the underlying causes of price fluctuations, such as economic indicators, monetary policy choices, geopolitical events, and market emotion. By examining the underlying elements that drive currency valuations, traders may make better decisions and anticipate prospective market shifts.

Economic indicators are a significant component of basic research since they provide important insights into an economy's health and performance. These indicators include GDP, inflation, employment, retail sales, manufacturing production, and trade balances. Traders regularly follow economic statistics to determine an economy's strength, appraise its growth prospects, and predict prospective monetary policy moves from central banks. Positive economic data releases often result in currency gain. In contrast, negative data releases can cause currency depreciation as market players modify their assumptions about future interest rates and economic development prospects.

Monetary policy choices by central banks are another critical component of fundamental research in forex trading. Central banks, including the Federal Reserve (Fed) in the United States, the European Central Bank (ECB) in the Eurozone, and the Bank of Japan (BOJ) in Japan, play critical roles in shaping monetary policy to achieve their respective economic goals, such as price stability, full employment, and long-term economic growth. Traders look at central bank comments, meeting minutes, and interest rate decisions to determine the direction and amount of monetary policy changes, which can significantly impact currency valuations and market sentiment.

Geopolitical events and tensions impact currency valuations and market sentiment, affecting investor confidence, risk appetite, and capital flows. Elections, geopolitical wars, trade disputes, and policy changes can all cause higher market volatility and uncertainty, causing traders to modify their holdings and risk exposures. Traders monitor geopolitical developments and news stories to forecast probable market reactions and capitalize on trading opportunities resulting from geopolitical events.

Market sentiment is another major factor influencing currency values and price movements in the forex market. Market sentiment reflects traders' and investors' collective psychology, including their opinions, attitudes, and expectations for future market circumstances. Positive emotion increases risk appetite and encourages investors to seek higher-yielding currencies. At the same time, negative sentiment may cause risk aversion and a flight to safe-haven assets like the US dollar, Japanese yen, and Swiss franc. Traders use sentiment indicators like the VIX volatility index, investor surveys, and positioning data to evaluate market sentiment and spot potential movements in investor behavior.

In addition to these core components, fundamental analysis considers other macroeconomic aspects like fiscal policy, geopolitical concerns, demographic trends, and structural changes in the global economy. By taking a complete approach to fundamental component analysis, traders can better understand currency valuations and market dynamics, allowing them to make more informed trading decisions and manage risk more efficiently. While fundamental analysis takes time, effort, and research, it gives traders a firm foundation for navigating the complicated and ever-changing forex market landscape. With meticulous investigation and a good grasp of essential elements, traders can obtain a competitive advantage and long-term success in forex trading.

Risk Management Strategies

Risk management tactics are critical components of successful forex trading because they assist traders in reducing possible losses, protecting money, and maintaining gains in the face of market uncertainty and volatility. Effective risk management includes detecting, assessing, and managing the hazards associated with trading operations, such as market, leverage, liquidity, and psychological risks. Traders can achieve long-term success in the dynamic and competitive forex market by employing effective risk management tactics that maximize their risk-reward ratio, maintain consistency in trading performance, and increase their chances of success.

Position sizing is a fundamental aspect of risk management in forex trading. It entails establishing the right size for each trade on the trader's account size, risk tolerance, and trading objectives. Position size tries to keep the amount of capital at risk on each trade to a predetermined percentage of the trader's account balance, which usually ranges between 1% and 3% for each trade. By following tight position sizing standards, traders can reduce the impact of losing trades on their overall account equity and avoid catastrophic losses that could deplete their trading capital.

Another critical risk management approach is to use stop-loss orders, which are established price levels at which traders quit losing trades to limit possible losses. Stop-loss orders allow traders to define their risk per trade and protect against lousy price fluctuations beyond their control. Traders should set stop-loss levels using technical analysis, support and resistance levels, volatility, and other pertinent indicators. This ensures that stop-loss orders are placed strategically to reflect the market's fundamental dynamics and trading objectives.

Furthermore, traders should diversify their portfolios across numerous currency pairings and assets to disperse risk and reduce the correlation between deals. Diversification entails trading a variety of currency pairings with distinct characteristics, such as significant pairs, minor pairs, and exotic pairs, as well as other asset classes, including stocks, commodities, and indexes. By diversifying their portfolios, traders can reduce the impact of adverse market fluctuations in any particular currency pair or asset and the danger of severe losses from concentrated positions.

Risk management also includes monitoring and managing leverage to minimize excessive risk exposure and margin calls. While leverage boosts earnings and losses in forex trading, it also raises the risk of severe drawdowns and account depletion if not employed correctly. To maintain risk control and protect their trading capital, traders should stick to conservative leverage levels like 1:10 or 1:20. Furthermore, traders should routinely review their margin levels and account equity to guarantee compliance with margin requirements and avoid margin calls, which could result in forced liquidation of holdings.

Psychological risk management is another essential part of good risk management in forex trading, as emotions like fear, greed, and overconfidence can cloud judgment and lead to irrational trade decisions. To negotiate the market's ups and downs, traders must adopt a disciplined trading attitude, stick to predefined trading plans and risk management guidelines, and acquire patience, resilience, and emotional stability. Furthermore, traders should avoid chasing losses, revenge trading, and making rash decisions, as these behaviors can increase losses and jeopardize long-term trading performance.

Finally, risk management tactics are essential for successful forex trading because they assist traders in navigating the market's intricacies and achieving their trading objectives while protecting money and adequately managing risk. Traders can improve their trading performance by implementing sound risk management practices such as position sizing, setting stop-loss orders, diversifying portfolios, managing leverage, and maintaining emotional discipline. While no risk management technique can eliminate all trading hazards, sound risk management can considerably increase a trader's capacity to resist market volatility and achieve long-term profitability.

Common Forex Trading Terms

In the fast-paced world of forex trading, traders must learn famous trading words to communicate effectively, accurately evaluate market information, and manage the complexity of the foreign exchange market. These phrases refer to diverse concepts, tactics, and strategies traders use to monitor market movements, execute transactions, and manage risk. By becoming acquainted with these words, traders can increase their trading expertise, make educated decisions, and improve overall trading performance.

One of the most basic ideas in forex trading is the currency pair, which reflects the exchange rate between two currencies. Each currency pair consists of a base currency and a quote currency, with the exchange rate reflecting the amount of the quote currency required to buy one unit of the base currency. For example, in the EUR/USD currency pair, the base currency is the euro (EUR), whereas the quote currency is the US dollar (USD). Currency pairs are classified as primary, minor, and exotic depending on liquidity, trading volume, and economic relevance.

Another prevalent term in forex trading is the spread, which is the difference between a currency pair's bid and ask prices. The bid price reflects the price at which traders can sell the base currency, whereas the asking price represents the price at which traders can buy it. The spread is usually measured in pips, with narrower spreads suggesting greater liquidity and lower trading costs. Traders should know spreads when executing trades, as bigger spreads can reduce profitability and raise transaction costs.

Another significant idea in forex trading is leverage, which allows traders to control more prominent positions in the market using less cash. Leverage is expressed as a ratio, such as 1:50 or 1:100, representing the capital required to initiate and sustain a trading position. For example, a leverage ratio of 1:50 means that a trader can hold a $50,000 position with only $1,000 cash. While leverage enhances earnings and losses, it raises the risk of severe drawdowns and margin calls if not appropriately managed.

Pip is a phrase used to describe the minor incremental movement in the price of a currency pair, which is usually equivalent to 0.0001 or 0.01 for most currency pairs. For example, if the EUR/USD currency pair goes from 1.2000 to 1.2001, it is considered to have moved one pip. Pips are used to calculate profit and loss, set stop-loss and take-profit levels, and evaluate the volatility and liquidity of currency pairs. Traders should know pip values and computations to minimize risk and establish proper trade parameters.

The margin is the capital needed to open and maintain a trading position in the forex market, expressed as a percentage of the total position size. Margin needs differ according to the leverage ratio and the broker's margin policy, with more excellent leverage ratios necessitating lower margin requirements and vice versa. Traders must maintain sufficient margin in their trading accounts to cover potential losses and prevent margin calls, which occur when account equity falls below the statutory margin level, forcing the broker to liquidate holdings.

Stop-loss and take-profit orders are risk management strategies that traders employ to reduce possible losses and lock in winnings. A stop-loss order is placed at a predetermined price level lower than the entry price for long positions and higher than the entry price for short positions, allowing traders to exit losing bets before incurring significant losses. A take-profit order, on the other hand, is set at a predefined price level higher than the entry price for long positions or lower than the entry price for short positions, allowing traders to exit successful trades and profit at advantageous price levels.

To summarize, understanding common forex trading phrases is critical for traders to manage the complexities of the foreign currency market and make sound trading selections. Currency pairs, spreads, leverage, pips, margin, stop-loss, and take-profit orders are all ideas that traders may learn about to increase their trading knowledge, risk management, and overall success. Furthermore, remaining current on new developments and trends in the forex market and constantly expanding their trading vocabulary can help traders stay competitive and adaptive in an ever-changing forex trading environment.

CHAPTER V

Developing a Winning Trading Strategy

Overview of Different Trading Styles

Creating a profitable trading strategy is essential to gaining success in the volatile and competitive world of forex trading. Traders use a variety of trading styles, each with its own set of traits, methodology, and risk profiles, to profit from market opportunities and meet their trading goals. Understanding the many trading styles available allows traders to choose the technique that best fits their personality, risk tolerance, and financial goals and design a winning strategy that meets their needs.

Day trading is a popular forex trading strategy involving starting and closing positions on the same day to profit from short-term price swings. Day traders use technical analysis, chart patterns, and intraday indicators to discover high-probability trading opportunities and execute transactions accurately and quickly. Day trading necessitates a high focus, discipline, and mental agility since traders must make quick judgments in a fast-paced market while managing risk properly to avoid substantial losses. While day trading can be highly profitable, it entails dangers such as higher transaction costs and probable volatility during intraday sessions.

Swing trading is another popular trading method that aims to capture medium-term price changes that last many days or weeks. Swing traders seek to capitalize on the momentum of trending markets and profit from price swings between support and resistance levels. Unlike day traders, swing traders maintain positions for extended periods, allowing them to profit from more significant price changes while minimizing the impact of intraday volatility and noise. Swing trading takes patience, discipline, and the ability to recognize market trends and reversals accurately. Traders frequently employ technical indicators, trend lines, and chart patterns to identify potential entry and exit points and manage risk effectively.

Position trading is a long-term strategy in which you maintain positions for weeks, months, or even years to profit from fundamental trends and macroeconomic factors. Position traders focus on capturing broader market patterns and economic cycles, allowing them to profit from large price movements over time. Position trading necessitates a thorough understanding of fundamental analysis, financial indicators, geopolitical events, and the capacity to weather short-term volatility and market noise. Traders must be patient, resilient, and disciplined when using position trading tactics, as positions might take time to unfold and yield gains.

Scalping is a high-frequency trading strategy in which a large number of deals are executed in a short time to profit from tiny price swings. Scalpers seek to capture small bits of price action, frequently using tight spreads, fast execution, and low-latency trading technologies to enter and leave positions quickly. Scalping necessitates tremendous discipline, focus, and risk management abilities since traders must be able to make split-second judgments while managing many trades simultaneously. Scalping can be highly profitable in turbulent and liquid markets but entails considerable dangers, such as increased transaction costs and slippage.

Algorithmic trading, often known as automated trading, is a trading strategy that uses computer algorithms to execute trades based on predefined criteria and rules automatically. Algorithmic traders utilize quantitative models, statistical analysis, and historical data to create strategies that capitalize on market inefficiencies and generate alpha. Algorithmic trading has various advantages, including speed, accuracy, and emotion-free execution; nonetheless, it necessitates significant programming abilities, a robust infrastructure, and ongoing monitoring and optimization. Traders must carefully create and backtest their algorithms to verify their efficacy and dependability in various market conditions.

To summarize, building a good trading strategy necessitates careful examination of the many trading styles available and their applicability to individual tastes, goals, and risk tolerances. Day trading, swing trading, position trading, scalping, and algorithmic trading are distinct trading styles with opportunities and obstacles. Understanding the characteristics, techniques, and risk profiles of various trading styles allows traders to create a cohesive and solid trading strategy that increases their chances of success in the volatile and competitive forex market. Furthermore, ongoing learning, practice, and adaptation are required to refine and optimize trading techniques and stay ahead of the curve in an ever-changing trading scene.

Building Your Trading Plan

Any trader hoping to succeed in the fast-paced, cutthroat world of forex trading must first create a trading plan. A trading plan provides a structured framework for making well-informed trading decisions and consistently achieving profitability by acting as a roadmap outlining a trader's objectives, goals, methods, and risk management guidelines. Traders can reduce emotional decision-making, uphold discipline, and improve their chances of success in the forex market by creating a thorough trading plan.

Establishing precise and quantifiable trading objectives and targets is the first stage in creating a trading plan. Whether it's to make money, increase capital, or become financially independent, traders should know why they trade and set measurable objectives that support their objectives. Setting attainable, time-bound, and realistic goals will help traders monitor their development and gauge their success over time. To safeguard their trading capital and lessen the effect of losses on their total account equity, traders should also prioritize capital preservation and risk management in their trading plan.

After determining their aims and goals, traders can create a trading strategy that fits their trading style, risk tolerance, and market preferences. Technical indicators, chart patterns, and other fundamental elements used to identify trading opportunities are all included in a trading strategy, specifying the parameters and guidelines for entering and exiting deals. Traders should do extensive research and backtesting to confirm their trading technique and ensure it works in various market conditions. Furthermore, traders should include methods in their plans to diversify their approach and adjust to shifting market conditions.

To guard against potential losses and maintain trading money, risk management is an essential part of any trading plan and should be carefully considered. To reduce exposure and successfully manage risk, traders should identify their level of risk tolerance and set risk management guidelines, such as position sizing, stop-loss thresholds, and maximum risk per transaction. Stop-loss orders serve as a means of reducing losses by automatically leaving losing transactions at predefined price points. At the same time, position sizing guarantees that traders only risk a limited portion of their trading money on each trade. Traders should also monitor the market and modify their risk management criteria to account for shifts in account equity and market conditions.

Setting rules and guidelines for trade management and decision-making is crucial to creating a trading plan. Based on their trading strategy, traders should specify the requirements for trade entrance, such as particular entry signals and confirmation factors. To lock in profits and reduce losses, traders can also specify criteria for trade exit, such as profit targets, trailing stops, and exit signals. By establishing explicit rules and standards for trade management, trade managers can lessen the influence of their emotions on their decisions and maintain discipline in their trading strategy.

Finally, traders should periodically examine and analyze their trading plan to determine areas for development and gauge its efficiency. This includes assessing trade data and statistics, evaluating trading performance, and spotting patterns or trends in trading activity. To modify their trading strategy, traders should also keep an eye on changes in the market, economic data, and geopolitical developments. Over time, traders can enhance their overall trading success and adjust to changing market conditions by consistently improving and refining their trading plans.

In summary, creating a trading plan is crucial for success in forex trading because it gives investors a disciplined framework for reaching their trading objectives and making well-informed judgments. A trading plan should include clear goals and targets, a well-defined trading strategy, strict risk management criteria, and protocols for trade management and decision-making. By sticking to their trading plan and exercising discipline, traders can better manage the intricacies of the forex market and raise their chances of long-term success and profitability.

Choosing the Right Timeframe

A key component of creating a profitable trading strategy in the forex market is selecting the appropriate timeframe. A timeframe is the duration of a candlestick or bar on a price chart, which can range from seconds to years. Timeframes are vital because they influence the frequency and length of trading opportunities. When choosing a timeframe that fits their trading aims and style, traders must consider their preferences, trading objectives, and risk tolerance.

Tick charts, one-minute charts, and five-minute charts are examples of shorter timeframes that offer traders a high degree of granularity and a thorough understanding of price movements and market dynamics. To take advantage of short-term trading opportunities and profit from intraday price changes, short-term traders—such as scalpers and day traders—often favor shorter periods. Shorter timescales, however, also call for quicker decision-making, quick reflexes, and the capacity to respond quickly to changes in the market. Shorter-term traders must be ready to monitor the market and move quickly to take advantage of vanishing chances.

On the other hand, longer durations, including hourly, daily, or weekly charts, provide a more comprehensive view of price trends and market movements. To capture more significant price moves and patterns that develop over several days, weeks, or even months, longer-term traders—such as swing and position traders—often favor longer horizons. Extended time intervals give traders more significant pricing information and mitigate the effects of transient volatility and market noise, facilitating more dependable signals and seamless trade execution. However, longer timeframes also call for more extraordinary patience because positions may need to be held for extended periods to earn profits, and trades may take longer.

The trader's technical analysis tools and trading technique also influence the timeframe chosen. Shorter periods are more suitable for some trading methods, such as scalping and day trading, which depend on accurate timing and prompt execution to profit from intraday price swings. These traders frequently utilize technical indicators to pinpoint entry and exit points and short-term trends, such as oscillators, moving averages, and support and resistance levels. On the other hand, longer timeframes are more appropriate for other trading methods like trend following and swing trading, which concentrates on capturing longer-term momentum shifts and more excellent price patterns. These traders frequently employ trend lines, Fibonacci retracements, and chart patterns to spot essential price levels and possible reversal or continuation patterns.

Additionally, traders ought to think about how trading volume and market liquidity will affect the timeframe they have selected. Reduced liquidity and increased volatility in shorter timeframes might result in wider spreads, slippage, and higher transaction costs. To mitigate these factors' adverse effects on trading success, traders using shorter timeframes must be aware of them and modify their trading tactics accordingly. Conversely, longer durations typically have lower volatility and better liquidity, which leads to tighter spreads and more steady price movements. These advantageous circumstances allow traders working longer to execute trades more precisely and effectively.

In summary, selecting the appropriate timeframe is essential for forex traders and significantly impacts trading performance. When choosing a timeframe that complements their trading style and objectives, traders must consider their preferences, trading goals, and risk tolerance. Traders must be ready to modify their methods and strategies according to the chosen timeframe and market conditions, whether trading on shorter timescales to profit from intraday price fluctuations or longer timeframes to capture more enormous price patterns. In the fast-paced and fiercely competitive forex market, traders can improve their chances of success and accomplish their trading goals by utilizing reliable trading techniques and the best timeframe selection.

Back testing and Optimization

Developing a solid and successful forex trading strategy requires both backtesting and optimization. Back testing assesses a trading strategy's performance and efficacy under previous market conditions by comparing it to prior pricing data. Before risking money in live trading, traders can backtest a trading strategy's profitability, risk-adjusted returns, and dependability under various market conditions. Traders can enhance their overall trading performance by identifying the strengths and shortcomings in their methods through back testing.

Traders can input their trading strategy rules and parameters into specialist software or trading platforms to do a backtest, which allows them to see how the strategy would have fared over historical data. To replicate trading activity, traders usually choose a period, such as a few months or years, and then apply their trading method to historical price data. To assess the strategy's efficacy and ascertain its suitability for real-time trading, traders examine critical performance indicators, including profit and loss (P&L), win rate, maximum drawdown, and risk-reward ratio, during the backtest.

After back testing, traders can optimize a trading strategy's performance and profitability. Optimization entails fine-tuning the strategy's parameters, such as entry and exit rules, take-profit and stop-loss levels, and position sizing to maximize profits and reduce risk.

Traders can systematically test various parameter combinations and determine the best settings for their strategy by using optimization techniques like parameter sweeps, genetic algorithms, or optimization algorithms.

When optimizing a trading strategy, traders should use caution, though, as over-optimization, also known as curve-fitting, can produce outcomes that are not representative of the actual state of the market. When traders over-optimize their strategies to fit historical data exactly, they create a technique that works well in historical testing but performs poorly in actual trading because of shifting market conditions. When developing trading strategies, traders should prioritize tactics that perform consistently under market conditions and concentrate on robustness and simplicity to prevent over-optimization.

To confirm that their optimized trading techniques work in actual trading situations, traders also need to validate them using out-of-sample testing. Out-of-sample testing involves applying the optimized technique to a different dataset of historical price data that wasn't used for the first backtest or optimization. Before implementing the approach in real-time trading, traders can confirm its stability and dependability and build confidence in its performance by testing it on unobserved data.

Traders should constantly monitor and assess their trading methods in addition to back testing and optimization to adjust to shifting market conditions and sustain optimal performance. Over time, market dynamics change, and strategies that are successful in one setting might be less successful in another. To maximize their tactics for the state of the market, traders should frequently assess their trading plans, examine their performance indicators, and make the required modifications.

In conclusion, developing a successful trading strategy for the forex market requires optimization and back testing. Using past price data for back testing, traders can optimize their tactics to optimize returns while minimizing risk, allowing them to develop stable and dependable trading techniques that perform well in various market scenarios. Before applying their optimized techniques in actual trading, traders should use caution to prevent over-optimization and confirm them through out-of-sample testing. In the volatile and competitive forex market, traders can create trading strategies that withstand the test of time and lead to long-term success with thorough testing, optimization, and monitoring.

Psychology of Forex Trading

In the volatile and fast-moving forex market, traders' success or failure is primarily determined by their understanding of the psychology of the game. Although technical research, fundamental analysis, and risk management are essential aspects of trading, attaining consistent profitability also requires an awareness of and capacity to control one's emotions and mindset. The psychology of trading includes various emotions, cognitive biases, and behavioral inclinations that affect trading performance and decision-making. To handle the ups and downs of the market and keep their cool under pressure, traders need to cultivate a disciplined and resilient mindset.

Fear, which can take many forms, including Fear of loss, FOMO, and error fear, is one of the primary emotions that traders have to deal with. Fear can immobilize traders, preventing them from taking calculated risks or carrying out their trading strategy. Traders need to learn how to control their Fear by putting long-term objectives ahead of short-term swings, admitting that losses are inevitable, and remaining confident in their trading technique.

Traders can acquire the resilience and mental toughness required to overcome obstacles and maintain discipline in their trading technique by admitting and facing their concerns.

Another strong emotion that can impair judgment and cause illogical decision-making in forex trading is greed. After a run of profitable transactions, traders could get overconfident or give in to the urge to chase profits and take unwarranted risks. But greed can also lead to rash trading decisions, excessive leverage, and deviations from a trading strategy, resulting in considerable losses. To combat greed and keep a logical and disciplined attitude toward trading, traders must develop humility, discipline, and self-awareness. Traders can lessen the adverse effects of greed on their trading performance by establishing reasonable goals, following risk management guidelines, and refraining from making snap judgments.

In the world of forex trading, patience is a virtue because profitable trading frequently entails waiting for the perfect opportunities to present themselves and using discipline when placing trades. During market consolidation or low volatility, traders may become frustrated, bored, and desperate for activity, forcing transactions or giving up on their plans. On the other hand, impatience might result in snap judgments and needless losses. Traders must develop patience by seeking high-probability trading opportunities that fit their risk tolerance and trading plan. Traders can avoid overtrading and prioritize quality over quantity in their trading activity by exhibiting patience and discipline.

The most crucial psychological quality for effective forex trading is discipline, which includes sticking to a trading plan, observing set norms and regulations, and executing deals consistently and impartially. In the face of difficulty or temptation, discipline calls for self-control, constancy, and adherence to predetermined risk management guidelines. Traders must establish and maintain a routine to prevent distractions and emotional outbursts that could impair their trading effectiveness. Traders can develop self-confidence and succeed in the long run in the forex market by remaining disciplined and consistent in their trading strategy.

In conclusion, the psychology of forex trading greatly influences trading performance and results. To preserve focus, discipline, and resilience in their trading endeavors, traders must be aware of and control their emotions, cognitive biases, and behavioral patterns. In the fast-paced and cutthroat world of foreign exchange trading, traders may successfully negotiate market obstacles, surpass psychological roadblocks, and consistently turn a profit by developing a disciplined and resilient mindset.

CHAPTER VI

Technical Analysis Techniques

Support and Resistance Levels

Technical analysis tools and techniques like trend lines, moving averages, Fibonacci retracements, and horizontal lines can determine support and resistance levels at significant price levels where the previous market movement has produced reversals or consolidation, horizontal support, and resistance levels form. Trend lines, which connect successive highs or lows to indicate support or resistance, are diagonal lines drawn on a price chart that can be used to determine the strength and direction of underlying trends. Moving averages can serve as dynamic support and resistance levels, giving a smoothed picture of price movements over time. Examples of such moving averages include the 50-day and 200-day moving averages. Based on the proportionate retracement of a previous price move, Fibonacci retracements, based on the Fibonacci sequence, can be used to assist in identifying possible support and resistance levels.

Support and resistance levels help traders decide where to enter and leave a trade, where to place a stop loss, and how to take profits. To establish long positions anticipating a price bounce or reversal, traders may search for bullish signs, such as bullish candlestick patterns or oversold circumstances, when prices are getting close to a support level. On the other hand, as prices get close to a resistance level, traders could search for negative indicators to take short positions in anticipation of a halt or reversal in the market, such as bearish candlestick patterns or overbought circumstances.

Furthermore, traders frequently place stop-loss orders below support levels for long positions and above resistance levels for short positions to limit potential losses. Support and resistance levels can serve as dynamic reference points for risk management. Furthermore, traders can use resistance and support levels to define profit objectives. When prices hit essential support or resistance levels, they can take partial or complete profits. In the forex market, traders can enhance their overall profitability by decreasing risk, increasing the precision of their trade inputs and exits, and utilizing support and resistance levels in their trading strategy.

Levels of support and resistance are dynamic and subject to fluctuation due to fluctuations in investor mood, supply and demand imbalances, and changes in market dynamics. It is advisable for traders to consistently observe levels of support and resistance and modify their trading approach to align with evolving market circumstances. Trend-following or breakout traders may have trading opportunities when they see breakouts above or below support or resistance levels, indicating the possibility of a trend continuance or reversal.

To sum up, technical analysis's foundational ideas of support and resistance levels offer essential insights into prospective price points where buying and selling pressure can converge in the currency market. Support and resistance levels are tools that traders use to manage risk, set profit targets, determine entry and exit points, and make well-informed trading decisions. In the fast-paced and cutthroat forex market, traders can improve their trading performance, lower risk, and raise their chances of success by using support and resistance levels in their trading strategy.

Trend Analysis

Trend analysis is an essential concept in technical analysis because it allows traders to predict the direction and strength of price movements in the forex market. Understanding market trends is vital to making effective trading decisions since they provide valuable information about potential entry and exit points and the overall market mood. Traders use various tools and tactics to analyze trends, including trend lines, moving averages, and trend indicators, to identify and profit from trend-following opportunities.

One of the most basic and widely used trend analysis techniques is drawing diagonal lines on a price chart to connect consecutive lows (uptrends) or highs (downtrends). Trend lines help traders visualize the direction and slope of price movements and indicate potential areas of support and resistance within a trend. Higher and lower lows indicate an uptrend, whereas lower highs and lows define a downtrend. Trend lines can act as dynamic support and resistance levels, allowing traders to mark entry and exit points and stop-loss and take-profit levels.

Moving averages are another standard trend analysis tool that provides traders with a smooth representation of price changes over a given period. The simple moving average (SMA) and exponential moving average (EMA) are popular moving averages for calculating an asset's average price over a predetermined number of periods. Moving averages are commonly used by traders to evaluate the direction of the current trend and to produce trade signals based on the crossover of shorter- and longer-term moving averages. A bullish crossing happens when a shorter-term moving average crosses above a longer-term moving average, signaling the possibility of an uptrend. A bearish crossing occurs when a shorter-term moving average crosses below a longer-term moving average, signaling a possible downward trend.

Furthermore, trend indicators such as the Average Directional Index (ADX) and Moving Average Convergence Divergence (MACD) can help traders predict the strength and velocity of market movements. The ADX indicator measures the strength of a trend on a scale of 0 to 100, with values greater than 25 indicating a strong trend and readings less than 25 indicating a weak trend. The MACD, on the other hand, consists of two moving averages, the MACD line, and the signal line, and it leverages their convergence and divergence to predict future trend reversals. Traders use trend indicators to confirm trend direction, evaluate trend strength, and anticipate potential trend reversals or continuations.

Traders employ several trend analysis techniques to identify and profit from trend-following opportunities in the forex market. Trend analysis enables traders to filter out noise and focus on high-probability trading opportunities corresponding to the current market trend. Traders can optimize their profits by identifying trends early on and riding them out. However, traders must exercise caution and use risk management strategies to decrease the risk of trend trading, such as false breakouts and trend reversals.

To recap, trend analysis is integral to technical analysis since it helps traders understand the direction and strength of price movements in the forex market. Traders use a variety of tools and strategies, including trend lines, moving averages, and trend indicators, to research trends and make informed trading decisions. Identifying and taking advantage of trend-following opportunities enables traders to enhance their trading performance, increase profitability, and achieve long-term success in the turbulent and competitive forex market.

Chart Patterns

Chart patterns are visual representations of price fluctuations on a Forex chart that traders use to spot prospective trades and forecast future price movements. These patterns occur as a function of market psychology, in which traders and investors respond to market dynamics and take positions based on their perceptions of value and market conditions. Chart patterns can be divided into two categories: continuation patterns and reversal patterns. Continuation patterns suggest a small stop in the prevailing trend before it restarts, whereas reversal patterns indicate a possible shift in the trend's direction.

The flag pattern is a popular continuation pattern comprising a solid price movement followed by a period of stabilization in a rectangular pattern resembling a flag. The flag pattern usually appears after a strong upward or downward trend and signifies a temporary stop or consolidation before the trend restarts. Traders frequently search for breakouts above or below the flag pattern to validate the persistence of the trend and enter trades in the current trend's direction.

Another standard continuation design is the pennant pattern, similar to the flag pattern but features a time of consolidation in the shape of a symmetrical triangle pattern resembling a pennant. The pennant pattern usually appears after a significant price movement and signifies a brief halt or consolidation before the trend restarts. Traders seek breakouts above or below the pennant pattern to confirm the trend's continuation and place trades in the same direction as the trend.

In addition to continuation patterns, traders employ reversal patterns to predict future trend reversals and capitalize on countertrend trading chances. The head and shoulders pattern is one of the most well-known reversal patterns. It consists of three peaks: a higher peak (the head) flanked by two smaller peaks (the shoulders) separated by two troughs. The head and shoulders pattern is often seen toward the end of an upswing and indicates a possible reversal into a downturn. Traders seek a fall below the pattern's neckline to confirm the reversal and enter short bets with lower price targets.

Another popular reversal pattern is the double top and double bottom pattern, which consists of two peaks (for a double top) or two troughs (for a double bottom) separated by a period of consolidation. The double-top pattern happens after an uptrend and indicates a potential reversal to a downtrend. In contrast, the double-bottom pattern occurs at the end of a downtrend, suggesting a potential upswing reversal. Traders wait for breakouts below or above the pattern's neckline (for a double top or double bottom) to confirm the reversal and enter trades in the new trend's direction.

Traders employ chart patterns to discover prospective trading opportunities, determine entry and exit points, and manage risk in the forex market. By spotting patterns and comprehending their ramifications, traders can make more accurate and confident trading decisions. However, traders must exercise caution and employ risk management measures to reduce the dangers of pattern trading, such as false breakouts and whipsaws. With practice and expertise, traders can become competent at detecting and trading chart patterns, improving their overall trading performance in the volatile and competitive forex market.

Fibonacci Retracement

The Fibonacci retracement is a standard technical analysis method traders use to identify probable support and resistance levels in the forex market. The technique is based on the Fibonacci sequence, a mathematical notion created by Italian mathematician Leonardo Fibonacci in the thirteenth century. The Fibonacci sequence is a set of numbers in which each number is the sum of the two numbers before it, beginning with 0 (0, 1, 1, 2, 3, 5, 8, 13, 21, etc.). The sequence provides the foundation for many mathematical correlations and patterns in nature, art, and financial markets.

In forex trading, Fibonacci retracement levels predict potential price retracements or pullbacks into a broader trend. Traders create Fibonacci retracement levels by connecting two major points on a price chart, usually a swing high and a swing low, and then using Fibonacci ratios to find probable retracement levels. The most popular Fibonacci ratios in forex trading are 23.6%, 38.2%, 50%, 61.8%, and 100%.

The 23.6% retracement level is the shallowest and is frequently used as a minor support or resistance level. Traders watch for potential reversal or continuation signals at the 38.2% retracement level, considered moderate retracement. The 50% retracement level signifies considerable retracement and is sometimes seen as a strong support or resistance level. The 61.8% retracement level, commonly known as the "golden ratio," is one of the most significant Fibonacci levels and is frequently used as a crucial support or resistance level. Finally, the 100% retracement level shows a complete retracement of the previous price movement and is a possible reversal signal.

Traders utilize Fibonacci retracement levels and other technical analysis tools and indicators to discover prospective trading opportunities and determine entry and exit points. Traders may search for confluence between Fibonacci retracement levels and other support and resistance levels, trend lines, or chart patterns to boost the likelihood of a successful trade. Furthermore, traders can employ Fibonacci retracement levels with momentum oscillators or candlestick patterns to confirm potential reversal or continuation indications.

One of Fibonacci retracement's primary advantages is its ability to detect possible support and resistance locations even in highly trending markets. When prices rise, traders can utilize Fibonacci retracement levels to find potential areas of support from which to enter long bets in the direction of the trend. When prices are heading lower, traders can utilize Fibonacci retracement levels to identify potential regions of resistance and enter short bets in the trend's direction.

However, it is crucial to remember that Fibonacci retracement levels are not failsafe and should be used with other technical analysis tools and risk management strategies. Like any other technical analysis technique, Fibonacci retracement levels are subjective and can fluctuate according to timing and market conditions. Traders should be wary of the possibility of false signals and whipsaws, particularly in choppy or volatile markets.

To summarize, Fibonacci retracement is a valuable technical analysis method traders use to identify probable regions of support and resistance in the forex market. Using Fibonacci ratios to significant price levels, traders can identify probable retracement levels within a more substantial trend and make sound trading decisions. While Fibonacci retracement levels are not perfect, they can provide valuable insights into market dynamics and assist traders in identifying high-probability trades. With practice and skill, traders can add Fibonacci retracement into their trading technique, improving their overall success in the volatile and competitive forex market.

Moving Averages

Moving averages are a popular technical indicator in forex trading that helps traders detect trends, filter out market noise, and make sound trading decisions. A moving average is calculated by charting an asset's average closing price on a price chart over a given period. The resulting line smoothes out price volatility, giving traders a better understanding of the underlying trend. Moving averages are classified into three types: simple moving averages (SMA), exponential moving averages (EMA), and weighted moving averages (WMA), each with unique characteristics and advantages.

Simple moving averages (SMA) are the most basic moving averages, established by adding an asset's closing prices over a given time and dividing by the number of periods. SMA assigns equal weight to each data point in the calculation, producing a smooth and easy-moving average line. SMAs are excellent for identifying long-term trends and support and resistance levels, but they may lag price changes, particularly in tumultuous markets.

Exponential moving averages (EMA) are similar to SMAs, but they give more weight to recent price data, making them more sensitive to price moves. EMAs are derived by assigning more weight to the most recent closing prices, resulting in a faster-moving average line that responds more swiftly to price changes. EMAs are very effective for short-term trading and detecting trend reversals or entry/exit points in tumultuous markets.

Weighted moving averages (WMAs) are a less prevalent sort of moving average in which each data point is assigned a variable weight in the calculation. Like EMAs, WMAs give more weight to more recent data points, but they employ a more complicated weighting scheme that can change depending on the trader's preferences. WMAs are beneficial for smoothing out price fluctuations and finding patterns in volatile or choppy markets, but they can be more difficult to calculate and comprehend than SMAs and EMAs.

Traders use moving averages to assess price patterns and make trading decisions. One typical approach is to use moving average crossovers, in which traders seek bullish (upward) or bearish (downward) crossings between shorter-term and longer-term moving averages to identify potential entry or exit positions. For example, a bullish crossing occurs when a shorter-term moving average crosses above a longer-term moving average, indicating a possible uptrend. In contrast, a bearish crossover occurs when a shorter-term moving average crosses below a longer-term moving average, indicating a potential downtrend.

Another popular strategy is to employ moving averages as dynamic support and resistance levels, with traders looking for price bounces or reversals as prices approach or cross a moving average line. For example, in an uptrend, traders may attempt to purchase when prices fall back to a rising moving average line, which they see as a potential support level. In contrast, during a downtrend, traders may try to sell when prices rebound to a declining moving average line, which they see as a possible resistance level.

Traders also use moving averages to determine the direction and strength of trends, with prices above a rising moving average considered bullish and prices below a falling moving average considered bearish. Traders can also employ numerous moving averages of varying lengths to confirm trend direction and eliminate false signals. For example, a trader may utilize a combination of short-term (e.g., 20-day) and long-term (e.g., 50-day) moving averages to identify the general trend direction and trade in that direction.

To summarize, moving averages are adaptable and extensively used technical indicators in forex trading that assist traders in detecting trends, filtering out market noise, and making informed trading decisions. Moving averages can analyze trends, determine support and resistance levels, and provide trading signals. With their simplicity and efficacy, moving averages continue to be a cornerstone of technical analysis and a crucial tool for traders navigating the volatile and competitive forex markets.

CHAPTER VII

Fundamental Analysis Fundamentals

Economic Indicators and Events

Economic indicators are statistical metrics used to assess a country's economic performance. They are divided into three types: leading, trailing, and coincident indicators. Stock market returns, business inventories, and new capital goods orders all predict future economic activity. Lagging measures, such as unemployment rates and business earnings, confirm previously observed trends and shifts. Coincident indicators, such as gross domestic product (GDP), industrial production, and retail sales, provide insight into the economy's current situation.

One of the most important economic indicators is GDP, which measures the total value of goods and services generated inside a country over a given period. A rising GDP signals economic expansion, which may result in a higher currency as investors seek to invest in an expanding economy. In contrast, a shrinking GDP can indicate economic difficulties, potentially leading to a weaker currency. Employment numbers, such as the non-farm payrolls report in the United States, are closely tied to GDP because they provide information about the health of the labor market and impact currency movements.

Inflationary factors are also important in the forex market. The Consumer Price Index (CPI) and the Producer Price Index (PPI) track changes in the pricing of products and services from the consumer and producer perspectives, respectively. High inflation can undermine a currency's value by reducing purchasing power, causing central banks to hike interest rates to control inflation. Higher interest rates attract foreign investment, resulting in a stronger currency. Conversely, low inflation may result in lower interest rates, thus devaluing the currency.

Interest rates are a fundamental economic indicator. Central banks, like the Federal Reserve, the European Central Bank, and the Bank of Japan, use benchmark interest rates to control monetary policy. Changes in interest rates can have an immediate and significant impact on currency values. Higher interest rates tend to attract foreign capital, increasing demand for the currency and its value. On the other hand, lower interest rates discourage investment and cause the currency to depreciate.

Trade balances and current account deficits or surpluses are both critical economic indicators. A country with a trade surplus (exports exceeding imports) typically strengthens its currency due to increased demand for its goods and services. In contrast, a trade deficit can weaken a currency by selling more of it to pay for imports. The current account, which includes trade balances, earnings on foreign investments, and transfer payments, provides a more comprehensive picture of a country's economic interactions with the rest of the world.

Staying updated with significant economic events, such as central bank meetings, geopolitical developments, and major economic changes, is crucial for maintaining control in the Forex market. Traders who are well-informed about central bank meetings, where monetary policy decisions are made, can anticipate and react to announcements concerning interest rate changes, quantitative easing initiatives, or other monetary policy tools. Similarly, being aware of geopolitical events like elections, trade disputes, and conflicts can help traders navigate uncertainty and volatility in the Forex market, making them feel more in control of their investments.

Central Bank Policies

Central bank policies play a critical role in shaping economic conditions, financial markets, and currency values in the forex market. Central banks are responsible for formulating and implementing monetary policies to achieve specific macroeconomic objectives, such as price stability, full employment, and sustainable economic growth. Central bank policies primarily focus on adjusting interest rates, managing money supply, and implementing unconventional measures, such as quantitative easing, to influence borrowing costs, inflation, and overall economic activity.

One of the primary tools used by central banks to implement monetary policy is the adjustment of interest rates. By raising or lowering interest rates, central banks can influence borrowing costs for businesses and consumers, affecting spending and investment decisions and ultimately impacting economic activity. For example, central banks may raise interest rates to curb inflationary pressures and cool down an overheating economy, or they may lower interest rates to stimulate borrowing and spending and support economic growth during periods of economic weakness.

Another key tool used by central banks is the management of money supply through open market operations, reserve requirements, and discount window lending. Central banks can expand or contract the money supply by buying or selling government securities in the open market, adjusting reserve requirements for commercial banks, or providing short-term liquidity through the discount window. By controlling the availability of credit and liquidity in the financial system, central banks can influence interest rates and overall economic activity.

In addition to conventional monetary policy tools, central banks may also implement unconventional measures, such as quantitative easing (QE), to address severe economic downturns or financial crises. Quantitative easing involves the central bank purchasing government bonds or other financial assets from the market to inject liquidity into the economy and lower long-term interest rates. By expanding its balance sheet and increasing the supply of money in circulation, the central bank aims to stimulate borrowing and investment, boost asset prices, and support economic recovery.

Traders closely monitor central bank policies and statements for clues about future monetary policy direction and potential market-moving events. Central bank meetings, interest rate decisions, and monetary policy statements are closely watched by traders for signals of potential changes in interest rates, policy outlook, and economic conditions. Traders analyze central bank communications, economic data releases, and market reactions to gauge the impact on currency markets and adjust their trading strategies accordingly.

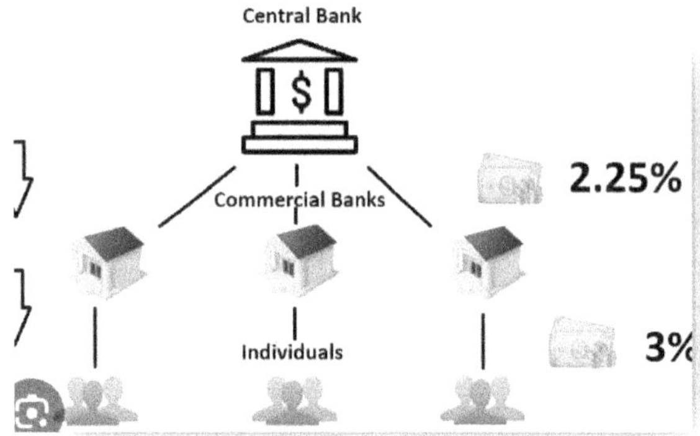

Central bank policies can also influence broader market sentiment and risk appetite, affecting asset prices across different financial markets. For example, accommodative monetary policy measures, such as quantitative easing, may boost investor confidence and lead to a rally in stock markets and riskier assets. Conversely, tightening monetary policy measures, such as interest rate hikes, may dampen investor sentiment and lead to a sell-off in risk assets as borrowing costs rise and economic growth prospects dim.

In conclusion, central bank policies play a crucial role in shaping economic conditions, financial markets, and currency values in the forex market. By adjusting interest rates, managing money supply, and implementing unconventional measures, central banks seek to achieve specific macroeconomic objectives and maintain stability in the financial system. Traders closely monitor central bank policies and statements for signals of potential market-moving events and adjust their trading strategies accordingly to capitalize on trading opportunities in the dynamic and competitive forex market.

Geopolitical Factors

Geopolitical factors encompass a broad range of political, social, and economic influences that can have significant impacts on global financial markets, including the forex market. These factors arise from interactions between nations, governments, international organizations, and geopolitical events and developments around the world. Geopolitical factors can create uncertainty, volatility, and risk in the forex market, as traders assess the potential implications of geopolitical events on economic growth, trade relations, and market sentiment.

One of the key geopolitical factors that traders monitor closely is geopolitical tensions and conflicts between nations or regions. Geopolitical tensions, such as trade disputes, territorial disputes, or military conflicts, can disrupt global supply chains, disrupt trade flows, and create uncertainty in financial markets. Traders often react to geopolitical tensions by seeking safe-haven assets, such as gold, the Swiss franc, or the Japanese yen, as a hedge against geopolitical risk. Additionally, geopolitical tensions can affect investor sentiment and risk appetite, leading to shifts in currency valuations and exchange rates.

Another important geopolitical factor is political instability and regime changes in countries or regions. Political instability, such as government corruption, social unrest, or political protests, can undermine investor confidence, disrupt economic activity, and lead to capital flight from affected countries. Traders closely monitor political developments and elections in key economies for potential implications on policy direction, economic reforms, and market stability. Political uncertainty can lead to heightened volatility and risk aversion in financial markets, impacting currency valuations and trading dynamics.

Moreover, geopolitical factors encompass geopolitical alliances and partnerships between nations, which can influence diplomatic relations, military alliances, and economic cooperation. Geopolitical alliances, such as military alliances, economic unions, or regional organizations, can promote stability, security, and economic prosperity in participating countries. Traders assess geopolitical alliances and partnerships for potential implications on regional security, trade relations, and market dynamics, as changes in geopolitical alliances can impact currency values and exchange rates.

Additionally, geopolitical factors include geopolitical events and crises, such as natural disasters, terrorist attacks, or pandemics, which can have immediate and far-reaching impacts on financial markets. Geopolitical events can disrupt supply chains, disrupt economic activity, and lead to heightened uncertainty and risk aversion among investors. Traders closely monitor geopolitical events for potential implications on market sentiment, risk appetite, and currency valuations, adjusting their trading strategies accordingly to mitigate risks and capitalize on trading opportunities.

In conclusion, geopolitical factors are important drivers of volatility, uncertainty, and risk in the forex market, as traders assess the potential implications of geopolitical events and developments on global financial markets. From geopolitical tensions and conflicts to political instability and trade disputes, geopolitical factors can create significant challenges and opportunities for traders navigating the dynamic and competitive forex market. By monitoring geopolitical developments closely and staying informed about geopolitical risks, traders can adapt their trading strategies and manage risks effectively to achieve success in the forex market.

Market Sentiment Analysis

Market sentiment analysis is a crucial aspect of trading in the forex market, as it provides insights into the collective psychology and mood of market participants. Market sentiment refers to the overall attitude or sentiment of traders and investors towards a particular currency pair, asset, or market as a whole. Market sentiment can be influenced by various factors, including economic data releases, geopolitical events, central bank policies, and investor perceptions of risk and uncertainty. Understanding market sentiment is essential for traders to anticipate market movements, identify trading opportunities, and manage risk effectively.

There are several methods used to analyze market sentiment in the forex market, including sentiment indicators, sentiment surveys, and sentiment analysis tools. Sentiment indicators, such as the Commitment of Traders (COT) report, provide insights into the positioning of institutional traders, such as hedge funds and commercial banks, in the futures market. The COT report shows the net long or short positions of large traders in various currency futures contracts, helping traders gauge market sentiment and potential trends.

Sentiment analysis tools use algorithms and artificial intelligence to analyze market sentiment based on news articles, social media posts, and other sources of information. These tools scrape and analyze large volumes of data to identify patterns, trends, and sentiment indicators that may impact market movements. Sentiment analysis tools can help traders identify market sentiment in real-time and make informed trading decisions based on sentiment signals.

Market sentiment can be classified into three main categories: bullish sentiment, bearish sentiment, and neutral sentiment. Bullish sentiment occurs when traders are optimistic about the prospects of a currency pair or asset, expecting prices to rise in the future. Bullish sentiment is typically associated with positive economic data releases, strong corporate earnings, or bullish technical indicators, and can lead to buying pressure and upward price movements in the market.

Conversely, bearish sentiment occurs when traders are pessimistic about the prospects of a currency pair or asset, expecting prices to decline in the future. Bearish sentiment is typically associated with negative economic data releases, weak corporate earnings, or bearish technical indicators, and can lead to selling pressure and downward price movements in the market.

Neutral sentiment occurs when traders are neither bullish nor bearish on a currency pair or asset, indicating a lack of strong conviction or consensus among market participants. Neutral sentiment may prevail during periods of uncertainty or consolidation in the market when traders are waiting for new information or developments to guide their trading decisions.

Traders use market sentiment analysis to gauge the strength and direction of market trends, identify potential reversal or continuation patterns, and make informed trading decisions. By understanding market sentiment and its drivers, traders can anticipate market movements, identify trading opportunities, and manage risk effectively in the dynamic and competitive forex market. However, it's essential for traders to exercise caution and use risk management techniques to mitigate the risks associated with trading based on market sentiment, as sentiment can change quickly and unpredictably in response to new information or developments.

Intermarket Analysis

Intermarket analysis is a comprehensive approach to trading that examines the relationships between different financial markets, including stocks, bonds, commodities, and currencies. The central premise of intermarket analysis is that these markets are interconnected and influence each other's movements, leading to correlations and trends that traders can exploit to make informed trading decisions. By analyzing the interrelationships between various asset classes, traders can gain valuable insights into broader market dynamics, anticipate potential market movements, and identify trading opportunities across different markets.

One of the key principles of intermarket analysis is the concept of intermarket correlations, which refers to the relationships between different asset classes and their impact on market movements. For example, there may be correlations between currencies and commodities, such as the Canadian dollar (CAD) and oil prices, or between stocks and bonds, such as the inverse relationship between stock prices and bond yields. By understanding these correlations, traders can anticipate how movements in one market may affect prices in another market and adjust their trading strategies accordingly.

Another important aspect of intermarket analysis is the study of asset class trends and market cycles. Different asset classes may exhibit similar or divergent trends and cycles, depending on various factors such as economic conditions, central bank policies, and investor sentiment. For example, during periods of economic expansion, stocks and commodities may rally together as investors seek higher returns, while bonds may underperform as interest rates rise. Conversely, during periods of economic contraction or uncertainty, investors may flock to safe-haven assets such as bonds and gold, leading to divergent trends across different asset classes.

Intermarket analysis also involves examining the impact of macroeconomic factors and geopolitical events on market movements. Economic indicators, central bank policies, geopolitical tensions, and other macroeconomic factors can influence investor sentiment, risk appetite, and market dynamics across different asset classes. For example, a hawkish central bank statement may strengthen a country's currency but weigh on stock prices, while a geopolitical crisis may boost demand for safe-haven assets such as gold and government bonds. By analyzing the interplay between macroeconomic factors and market movements, traders can gain insights into potential market trends and trading opportunities.

Traders use various tools and techniques to conduct intermarket analysis, including chart analysis, technical indicators, and quantitative models. Chart analysis involves visually inspecting price charts of different asset classes to identify patterns, trends, and correlations. Technical indicators, such as moving averages, relative strength index (RSI), and correlation coefficients, can help traders quantify and analyze intermarket relationships and trends. Quantitative models, such as econometric models or neural networks, can analyze large datasets and identify complex interrelationships between different markets and factors.

In conclusion, intermarket analysis is a powerful approach to trading that examines the relationships between different financial markets, sectors, and asset classes. By analyzing intermarket correlations, sector rotation patterns, asset class trends, and macroeconomic factors, traders can gain valuable insights into broader market dynamics and identify trading opportunities across different markets. Intermarket analysis allows traders to anticipate potential market movements, manage risk effectively, and adapt their trading strategies to changing market conditions in the dynamic and interconnected world of finance.

CHAPTER VIII

Advanced Trading Strategies

Scalping Techniques

Scalping is an advanced trading strategy employed by traders seeking to capitalize on small price movements in the forex market. The primary goal of scalping is to make a high volume of small profits throughout the trading session by entering and exiting trades rapidly. Scalping requires a high level of discipline, precision, and risk management, as traders aim to capture small price fluctuations while minimizing exposure to market volatility and adverse price movements. Scalping techniques typically involve trading on short-term timeframes, such as one-minute or five-minute charts, and utilizing technical indicators, chart patterns, and price action analysis to identify entry and exit points.

One of the key principles of scalping is to take advantage of market inefficiencies and liquidity imbalances to execute trades quickly and profitably. Scalpers often focus on highly liquid currency pairs with tight spreads and low transaction costs, such as EUR/USD or USD/JPY, to maximize trading opportunities and minimize trading costs. By trading during periods of high trading volume and market activity, scalpers can capitalize on short-term price movements and liquidity fluctuations to generate profits.

Scalping techniques typically involve using a combination of technical indicators and chart patterns to identify short-term trading opportunities. Common technical indicators used by scalpers include moving averages, stochastic oscillators, relative strength index (RSI), and Bollinger Bands, among others. These indicators help traders identify overbought or oversold conditions, trend reversals, and potential entry and exit points for trades. Scalpers also use chart patterns, such as triangles, flags, and pennants, to identify potential breakout or reversal opportunities and enter trades accordingly.

Execution speed and efficiency are paramount in scalping, as trades are entered and exited within seconds or minutes. Scalpers often use direct market access (DMA) or electronic communication networks (ECNs) to execute trades with minimal latency and slippage. By using advanced trading platforms and technology, scalpers can reduce execution times and improve order fill rates, increasing the likelihood of successful trades and maximizing profitability.

Scalping requires a high level of concentration and focus, as traders must monitor multiple currency pairs and markets simultaneously to identify trading opportunities and execute trades quickly. Scalpers often employ a disciplined trading routine and strict trading rules to maintain consistency and avoid emotional decision-making. By adhering to predefined trading strategies and risk management rules, scalpers can minimize the impact of emotions on their trading decisions and maintain a disciplined approach to trading.

In conclusion, scalping is an advanced trading strategy that involves making a high volume of small profits by capitalizing on short-term price movements in the forex market. Scalping requires a high level of discipline, precision, and risk management, as traders aim to execute trades quickly and efficiently while minimizing exposure to market volatility and adverse price movements. By employing advanced trading techniques, technical analysis tools, and strict risk management rules, scalpers can maximize profitability and achieve success in the dynamic and competitive world of forex trading.

Day Trading Strategies

Day trading is a trading strategy that involves buying and selling financial assets within the same trading day to capitalize on short-term price movements. Day traders aim to profit from intraday fluctuations in asset prices, taking advantage of small price movements and volatility in the market. Day trading requires quick decision-making, discipline, and risk management, as traders seek to execute multiple trades throughout the trading session while minimizing losses and maximizing gains.

One of the key principles of day trading is to focus on highly liquid assets with tight spreads and high trading volumes to ensure ease of entry and exit. Day traders often focus on liquid stocks, forex pairs, or futures contracts that exhibit significant intraday volatility and provide ample trading opportunities. By trading highly liquid assets, day traders can execute trades quickly and efficiently, minimizing slippage and transaction costs.

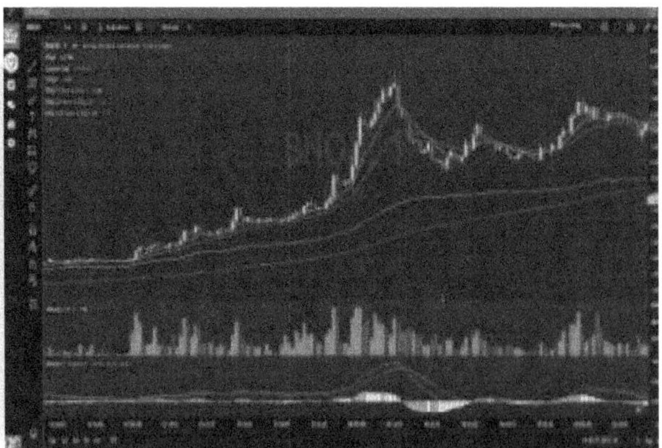

Day trading strategies vary widely depending on the trader's trading style, risk tolerance, and market conditions. Some common day trading strategies include momentum trading, trend following, and range trading. Momentum trading involves buying or selling assets based on the strength and velocity of price movements, typically in the direction of the prevailing trend. Trend-following strategies involve identifying and trading with the underlying trend, buying on pullbacks in uptrends and selling on rallies in downtrends. Range trading strategies involve buying near support levels and selling near resistance levels in sideways or ranging markets.

Technical analysis plays a significant role in day trading, as traders use price charts, technical indicators, and chart patterns to identify trading opportunities and make informed decisions. Common technical indicators used by day traders include moving averages, relative strength index (RSI), stochastic oscillators, and volume indicators. These indicators help traders identify overbought or oversold conditions, trend reversals, and potential entry and exit points for trades. Day traders also use chart patterns, such as triangles, flags, and head and shoulders patterns, to identify potential breakout or reversal opportunities and enter trades accordingly.

Execution speed and efficiency are paramount in day trading, as traders aim to capitalize on short-term price movements and intraday volatility. Day traders often use direct market access (DMA) or electronic communication networks (ECNs) to execute trades with minimal latency and slippage. By using advanced trading platforms and technology, day traders can reduce execution times and improve order fill rates, increasing the likelihood of successful trades and maximizing profitability.

In conclusion, day trading is a trading strategy that involves buying and selling financial assets within the same trading day to capitalize on short-term price movements. Day traders aim to profit from intraday fluctuations in asset prices, using a variety of strategies, technical analysis tools, and risk management techniques. By focusing on highly liquid assets, employing disciplined trading strategies, and leveraging advanced technology, day traders can navigate the dynamic and competitive world of day trading and achieve success in the financial markets.

Swing Trading Approaches

Swing trading is a popular trading strategy that aims to capture short to medium-term price movements in financial markets. Unlike day trading, which involves buying and selling assets within the same trading day, swing trading typically involves holding positions for several days to weeks to take advantage of price swings or "swings" in the market. Swing traders aim to profit from both upward and downward price movements by entering trades at key support or resistance levels and riding the price momentum as it develops.

One of the key principles of swing trading is identifying and trading with the prevailing market trend. Swing traders typically look for assets that are trending strongly in one direction, either upward (bullish) or downward (bearish) and aim to enter trades in the direction of the trend. Trend-following indicators, such as moving averages, trendlines, and momentum oscillators, are commonly used by swing traders to identify the direction and strength of the trend and to confirm potential entry and exit points for trades.

Another approach to swing trading is mean reversion trading, which involves identifying overextended price movements and betting on a reversal or "mean reversion" back to the average or mean price. Mean reversion traders look for assets that have deviated significantly from their long-term average prices and enter trades with the expectation that prices will revert back to the mean. Mean reversion strategies often involve using technical indicators, such as Bollinger Bands, stochastic oscillators, or relative strength index (RSI), to identify overbought or oversold conditions and potential reversal points.

Swing traders also employ various technical analysis tools and chart patterns to identify potential trading opportunities and confirm entry and exit points for trades. Common chart patterns used by swing traders include triangles, flags, pennants, and double tops/bottoms, among others. These patterns can provide valuable insights into market sentiment, price action, and potential trend reversals, helping swing traders make informed trading decisions.

Execution timing is essential in swing trading, as traders aim to enter trades at optimal entry points and ride the price momentum as it develops. Swing traders often wait for confirmation signals, such as trendline breaks, moving average crossovers, or chart pattern breakouts, before entering trades to increase the probability of success. By waiting for confirmation signals, swing traders can reduce the risk of false breakouts or trend reversals and increase the likelihood of profitable trades.

In conclusion, swing trading is a versatile trading strategy that aims to capture short to medium-term price movements in financial markets. By identifying and trading with the prevailing market trend, employing mean reversion strategies, and using technical analysis tools and chart patterns, swing traders can identify potential trading opportunities and make informed trading decisions. With proper risk management techniques and disciplined execution, swing traders can navigate the dynamic and competitive world of swing trading and achieve success in the financial markets.

Carry Trade Strategy

The carry trade strategy is a popular trading approach in the forex market that involves borrowing funds in a low-interest-rate currency and investing in a high-interest-rate currency to capture the interest rate differential or "carry" between the two currencies. The primary goal of the carry trade is to profit from the interest rate differential while also potentially benefiting from exchange rate movements. The carry trade strategy is based on the concept of borrowing funds at a low cost and investing them in assets that offer higher returns, thereby generating a positive yield or profit.

One of the key principles of the carry trade strategy is to identify currency pairs with significant interest rate differentials and stable exchange rate dynamics. Carry trade opportunities typically arise in currency pairs where there is a substantial interest rate gap between the two countries' central banks. Traders look for currencies with relatively high interest rates, such as the Australian dollar (AUD), New Zealand dollar (NZD), or emerging market currencies, and borrow funds in low-interest-rate currencies, such as the Japanese yen (JPY) or Swiss franc (CHF), to fund their carry trades.

The carry trade strategy can be implemented using various financial instruments, including spot forex contracts, currency futures, or currency exchange-traded funds (ETFs). Traders typically enter carry trades by buying the high-yielding currency against the low-yielding currency, aiming to hold the position for an extended period to capture the interest rate differential. In addition to earning interest income from the positive carry, traders may also benefit from capital appreciation if the high-yielding currency appreciates against the low-yielding currency.

Political and economic factors can also influence the success of carry trades. Traders must carefully monitor central bank policies, economic indicators, and geopolitical events that may impact interest rates and exchange rates in the countries of the currency pairs being traded. Changes in monetary policy, economic data releases, or geopolitical tensions can affect market sentiment, risk appetite, and currency valuations, potentially impacting the profitability of carry trades.

Despite the potential risks associated with the carry trade strategy, it remains popular among traders seeking to generate consistent returns from interest rate differentials and exchange rate movements. Carry trades can offer attractive returns in environments of low volatility and stable interest rates, providing traders with opportunities for income generation and portfolio diversification. However, traders must exercise caution and implement proper risk management techniques to mitigate the risks associated with carry trades and ensure long-term profitability.

In conclusion, the carry trade strategy is a popular trading approach in the forex market that aims to profit from interest rate differentials between currencies. By borrowing funds in low-interest-rate currencies and investing in high-interest-rate currencies, traders can capture the interest rate differential or "carry" while also potentially benefiting from exchange rate movements. While carry trades can offer attractive returns, traders must carefully manage risk and monitor market conditions to ensure the success of their carry trade positions. With proper risk management techniques and a thorough understanding of market dynamics, traders can effectively implement the carry trade strategy and achieve success in the dynamic and competitive world of forex trading.

Hedging Strategies

Hedging strategies are risk management techniques employed by traders and investors to protect against potential losses from adverse market movements. The primary goal of hedging is to reduce or eliminate the impact of market volatility and uncertainty on portfolio performance while preserving capital and mitigating downside risk. Hedging strategies involve taking offsetting positions in related or correlated assets to offset potential losses in the primary position. Hedging can be achieved using various financial instruments, including derivatives such as options, futures, forwards, and swaps, as well as by diversifying across different asset classes, currencies, or geographic regions.

One of the most common hedging strategies is using derivatives such as options to protect against adverse price movements in the underlying asset. For example, an investor holding a portfolio of stocks may purchase put options to hedge against potential downside risk in the stock market. Put options give the holder the right to sell the underlying asset at a predetermined price (the strike price) within a specified period (the expiration date). By purchasing put options, the investor can protect against losses if the stock market declines, as the put options will increase in value as the stock prices fall, offsetting losses in the stock portfolio.

Another hedging strategy is using futures contracts to hedge against price fluctuations in commodities, currencies, or financial assets. For example, a multinational corporation may use currency futures contracts to hedge against currency exchange rate risk when conducting international trade. By entering into currency futures contracts to buy or sell foreign currencies at predetermined exchange rates, the corporation can lock in future currency exchange rates and protect against adverse movements in exchange rates that could impact the value of its international transactions.

Hedging can also be achieved through diversification, which involves spreading investments across different asset classes, sectors, or geographic regions to reduce overall portfolio risk. By diversifying their portfolios, investors can reduce the impact of adverse market movements in one asset or market on their overall portfolio performance. For example, an investor may hold a diversified portfolio of stocks, bonds, commodities, and real estate to spread risk and protect against losses from any single asset class or market.

Options strategies, such as collars, straddles, and strangles, are also commonly used for hedging purposes. Collar strategies involve simultaneously buying a protective put option and selling a covered call option on an underlying asset to limit downside risk while generating income from the sale of the call option. Straddle strategies involve buying both a put option and a call option on the same underlying asset with the same strike price and expiration date to profit from significant price movements in either direction. Strangle strategies involve buying out-of-the-money put and call options on the same underlying asset with different strike prices to profit from volatility while limiting downside risk.

In conclusion, hedging strategies are risk management techniques used by traders and investors to protect against potential losses from adverse market movements. Hedging can be achieved using various financial instruments, including derivatives, diversification, and options strategies. While hedging can help mitigate downside risk and preserve capital, it also comes with costs and limitations, and may not fully protect against losses in all market conditions. Traders and investors must carefully assess their risk tolerance, investment objectives, and market conditions when implementing hedging strategies to effectively manage risk and achieve their financial goals.

CHAPTER IX

Risk Management and Capital Preservation

Position Sizing

One of the fundamental principles of position sizing is the concept of risk per trade, which refers to the maximum amount of capital that a trader is willing to risk on each individual trade. Risk per trade is typically expressed as a percentage of the trading account balance, commonly referred to as the risk percentage or risk tolerance. For example, a trader may decide to risk 1% of their trading account balance on each trade, meaning that if the trade results in a loss, the maximum drawdown on the account will be limited to 1% of the total account balance.

Determining the appropriate risk per trade involves assessing factors such as the trader's risk tolerance, trading strategy, and market conditions. Traders with a higher risk tolerance or those trading in more volatile markets may opt for a higher risk percentage, while conservative traders or those trading in less volatile markets may prefer a lower risk percentage. Additionally, the risk per trade should be aligned with the trader's overall risk management strategy and trading objectives, ensuring that losses are kept within acceptable limits and do not jeopardize the long-term viability of the trading account.

Once the risk per trade has been established, traders can calculate the position size for each trade based on the stop-loss level and the distance to the stop-loss order. Position size is calculated by dividing the risk per trade by the distance from the entry price to the stop-loss level, expressed in terms of the number of pips or price units. For example, if a trader is risking 1% of their account balance on a trade with a stop-loss distance of 50 pips, the position size would be calculated as follows: position size = (risk per trade / stop-loss distance) * pip value.

Implementing proper position sizing techniques can help traders manage risk effectively and preserve capital during periods of market volatility and uncertainty. By limiting the size of each trade relative to the trading account balance, traders can protect themselves against large losses and maintain consistency in their trading results over time. Additionally, position sizing allows traders to scale their positions based on market conditions and trading opportunities, optimizing risk-reward ratios and maximizing the potential return on investment.

In addition to calculating position sizes based on risk per trade, traders may also consider incorporating other risk management techniques, such as diversification, correlation analysis, and portfolio optimization, into their overall risk management strategy. Diversification involves spreading investments across different asset classes, markets, or trading strategies to reduce overall portfolio risk and minimize the impact of adverse market movements on portfolio performance. Correlation analysis involves assessing the relationships between different assets or markets to identify potential sources of risk and opportunities for hedging or diversification. Portfolio optimization involves allocating capital to different assets or trading strategies based on risk-return profiles, expected returns, and correlation coefficients to achieve the optimal balance between risk and return.

In conclusion, position sizing is a critical aspect of risk management and capital preservation in trading. By determining the appropriate risk per trade, calculating position sizes based on stop-loss levels, and incorporating other risk management techniques into their trading strategies, traders can effectively manage risk, protect capital, and improve the consistency of their trading results. Position sizing allows traders to control risk while maximizing the potential return on investment, enhancing their ability to achieve long-term success in the dynamic and competitive world of trading.

Stop Loss and Take Profit Orders

Stop-loss and take-profit orders are essential tools used by traders to manage risk and protect profits in the financial markets. A stop-loss order is an instruction given to a broker to automatically sell a security when it reaches a specified price level, limiting the trader's potential loss on the trade. Take-profit orders, on the other hand, are instructions to sell a security when it reaches a predetermined price level to lock in profits from a trade. These orders are crucial components of risk management strategies and help traders implement disciplined and systematic approaches to trading.

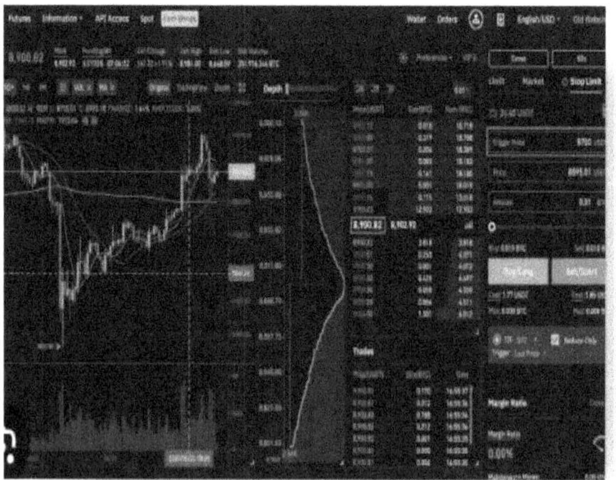

Stop-loss orders serve as a safety net for traders, helping them to limit potential losses and protect their capital in case the market moves against their position. By setting a stop-loss order at a predefined price level, traders can exit losing trades before significant losses occur, preserving their trading capital and minimizing the impact of adverse market movements. Stop-loss orders can be placed at various price levels, including below the entry price for long positions and above the entry price for short positions, depending on the trader's risk tolerance and trading strategy.

Take-profit orders, on the other hand, are used to lock in profits and exit winning trades at predetermined price levels. By setting a take-profit order at a target price level, traders can ensure that they capture profits from a trade before the market reverses and erodes their gains. Take-profit orders can be placed at various price levels, including above the entry price for long positions and below the entry price for short positions, depending on the trader's profit targets and trading strategy.

Implementing stop-loss and take-profit orders allows traders to remove emotion from their trading decisions and adhere to predefined risk management rules. By setting these orders in advance, traders can avoid the temptation to hold onto losing trades in the hope that the market will reverse in their favor or to prematurely exit winning trades out of fear of losing profits. Stop-loss and take-profit orders help traders maintain discipline and consistency in their trading, reducing the likelihood of emotional decision-making and improving overall trading performance.

One of the key benefits of using stop-loss and take-profit orders is that they allow traders to automate their trading process and manage their positions more efficiently. Instead of constantly monitoring the markets and manually entering and exiting trades, traders can set stop-loss and take-profit orders in advance and let the orders execute automatically when the specified price levels are reached. This not only saves time and effort but also helps traders avoid missed opportunities or costly mistakes that can occur due to human error or emotional bias.

While stop-loss and take-profit orders are powerful risk management tools, traders should be aware of their limitations and potential drawbacks. Stop-loss orders are not guaranteed to be executed at the specified price level, especially in fast-moving or illiquid markets, and may result in slippage or partial fills. Take-profit orders may also cause traders to miss out on potential profits if the market continues to move in their favor after the order is executed. Additionally, traders should carefully consider the placement of stop-loss and take-profit orders to ensure they are aligned with their trading strategy and risk tolerance.

In conclusion, stop-loss and take-profit orders are essential tools used by traders to manage risk and protect profits in the financial markets. These orders help traders limit potential losses and lock in profits from their trades, allowing them to implement disciplined and systematic approaches to trading. By setting stop-loss and take-profit orders in advance, traders can remove emotion from their trading decisions, maintain discipline, and improve overall trading performance. While stop-loss and take-profit orders have limitations, they are valuable components of risk management strategies and essential for long-term success in trading.

Diversification Strategies

Diversification strategies are fundamental principles used by investors to manage risk and optimize returns by spreading investments across a variety of asset classes, sectors, industries, and geographic regions. The core idea behind diversification is to reduce the overall risk of a portfolio by investing in a mix of assets that are not closely correlated with each other. By diversifying their investments, investors can minimize the impact of adverse market movements in one asset or market on their overall portfolio performance, while also maximizing the potential for long-term growth and capital preservation.

One of the most common diversification strategies is asset allocation, which involves spreading investments across different asset classes, such as stocks, bonds, commodities, real estate, and cash equivalents. Each asset class has unique characteristics and responds differently to changes in market conditions, economic factors, and geopolitical events. By allocating capital to a mix of asset classes with varying risk-return profiles, investors can reduce overall portfolio risk and increase the likelihood of achieving their investment objectives.

Within each asset class, investors can further diversify their portfolios by spreading investments across different sectors, industries, and companies. For example, within the stock market, investors can allocate capital to companies operating in various sectors such as technology, healthcare, finance, consumer goods, and industrials. By diversifying across sectors, investors can reduce the impact of sector-specific risks and capitalize on opportunities for growth in different areas of the economy.

Geographic diversification is another important aspect of diversification strategies, as it involves spreading investments across different geographic regions and markets. By investing in assets from different countries and regions, investors can reduce exposure to country-specific risks, such as political instability, regulatory changes, and currency fluctuations. Geographic diversification allows investors to benefit from growth opportunities in emerging markets while also mitigating the impact of economic downturns or geopolitical tensions in specific regions.

Diversification strategies can also be applied within specific asset classes, such as fixed income securities and real estate. Within the fixed income market, investors can diversify their bond portfolios by investing in bonds with different maturities, credit qualities, and issuers. Similarly, in real estate investing, investors can diversify their property portfolios by investing in properties across different locations, property types, and market segments.

While diversification strategies can help investors reduce portfolio risk and enhance long-term returns, it is essential to note that diversification does not eliminate all investment risk. Certain risks, such as systemic risk, market risk, and geopolitical risk, cannot be diversified away and affect all investments to some extent. Additionally, over-diversification can dilute potential returns and increase portfolio complexity and management costs. Therefore, investors should carefully balance the benefits of diversification with their investment goals, risk tolerance, and time horizon when constructing their portfolios.

In conclusion, diversification strategies are essential principles used by investors to manage risk and optimize returns in the financial markets. By spreading investments across a mix of asset classes, sectors, industries, and geographic regions, investors can reduce portfolio risk, enhance long-term growth potential, and achieve their investment objectives. Diversification allows investors to capitalize on opportunities for growth while also mitigating the impact of adverse market movements and economic events. With proper diversification strategies in place, investors can build resilient portfolios that withstand market volatility and deliver consistent returns over time.

Managing Leverage

Managing leverage is a crucial aspect of trading and investing in financial markets, as it can significantly amplify both potential gains and losses. Leverage allows traders to control larger positions in the market with a smaller amount of capital, thereby magnifying the impact of price movements on their trading accounts. While leverage can enhance profitability by increasing the potential return on investment, it also exposes traders to higher levels of risk and can result in substantial losses if not managed properly.

One of the key principles of managing leverage is understanding the concept of leverage ratio, which represents the amount of capital borrowed from a broker to control a larger position in the market. Leverage is typically expressed as a ratio, such as 50:1 or 100:1, indicating the amount of leverage provided by the broker relative to the trader's capital. For example, with a leverage ratio of 100:1, a trader can control a position worth $100,000 with just $1,000 of capital.

While leverage can magnify potential profits, it also increases the potential for losses, as traders are exposed to greater market risk. Therefore, it is essential for traders to use leverage judiciously and apply risk management techniques to protect their capital. One approach to managing leverage is to limit the size of leveraged positions relative to the trading account balance. By adhering to conservative leverage ratios and avoiding excessive leverage, traders can reduce the impact of adverse market movements on their trading accounts and mitigate the risk of margin calls or account liquidation.

Another important aspect of managing leverage is setting stop-loss orders to limit potential losses on leveraged trades. Stop-loss orders allow traders to define their maximum acceptable loss on a trade and automatically exit the position if the market moves against them beyond a certain point. By setting stop-loss orders at predetermined levels, traders can control risk and protect their capital from excessive losses resulting from leveraged positions.

It is also essential for traders to understand the terms and conditions of leverage offered by their brokers and the potential risks associated with leveraged trading. Brokers may impose margin requirements, maintenance margin levels, and margin calls to manage the risk of leveraged positions and protect their interests. Traders should carefully read and understand the margin agreement and risk disclosure statement provided by their brokers and assess their risk tolerance and financial situation before engaging in leveraged trading.

In conclusion, managing leverage is a critical aspect of trading and investing in financial markets. While leverage can enhance profitability by amplifying potential gains, it also exposes traders to higher levels of risk and potential losses. By using leverage judiciously, applying risk management techniques, and understanding the terms and conditions of leveraged trading, traders can protect their capital, minimize losses, and improve their chances of success in the dynamic and competitive world of financial markets.

Dealing with Emotions and Stress

Dealing with emotions and stress is a critical aspect of successful trading and investing in financial markets. The fast-paced and unpredictable nature of the markets can evoke a range of emotions, including fear, greed, anxiety, and euphoria, which can influence decision-making and impact trading performance. Managing emotions and stress effectively is essential for maintaining discipline, making rational decisions, and achieving long-term success in the dynamic and competitive world of trading.

One of the first steps in dealing with emotions and stress is developing self-awareness and recognizing the emotions that arise during trading. By acknowledging and understanding their emotions, traders can gain insight into their thought processes and behavior patterns, enabling them to identify potential triggers and develop strategies to manage them effectively. Techniques such as mindfulness meditation, journaling, and self-reflection can help traders cultivate self-awareness and develop emotional intelligence, allowing them to respond to market events with greater composure and clarity.

Another key aspect of dealing with emotions and stress is developing a disciplined trading plan and sticking to it consistently. A well-defined trading plan outlines specific entry and exit criteria, risk management rules, and profit targets, providing traders with a clear roadmap for navigating the markets. By following their trading plan religiously and avoiding impulsive decisions based on emotions, traders can maintain discipline and avoid costly mistakes that can result from emotional trading.

Developing resilience is another important aspect of dealing with emotions and stress in trading. Resilience refers to the ability to bounce back from setbacks, adapt to changing circumstances, and maintain a positive mindset in the face of adversity. Trading can be a challenging and unpredictable endeavor, and traders are bound to experience losses and setbacks along the way. By cultivating resilience and adopting a growth mindset, traders can view setbacks as learning opportunities and use them to refine their trading strategies and improve their skills over time.

Effective stress management techniques can also help traders cope with the pressures of trading and maintain emotional balance. Regular exercise, healthy eating, adequate sleep, and relaxation techniques such as deep breathing exercises, yoga, and meditation can help reduce stress levels and promote mental and emotional well-being. Taking breaks from trading, spending time with loved ones, and pursuing hobbies and interests outside of trading can also provide perspective and balance, helping traders maintain a healthy work-life balance and avoid burnout.

Building a supportive network of fellow traders, mentors, and coaches can also be beneficial for dealing with emotions and stress in trading. Sharing experiences, seeking advice, and receiving encouragement from others in the trading community can provide valuable support and validation, helping traders navigate the ups and downs of trading with greater resilience and confidence. Participating in trading forums, attending trading seminars, and joining trading communities can provide opportunities for networking and collaboration, fostering a sense of belonging and camaraderie among traders.

In conclusion, dealing with emotions and stress is an essential aspect of successful trading and investing in financial markets. By developing self-awareness, maintaining discipline, implementing robust risk management techniques, cultivating resilience, and practicing effective stress management techniques, traders can cope with the pressures of trading and maintain emotional balance in the face of market volatility and uncertainty. With a clear trading plan, a positive mindset, and a supportive network, traders can navigate the challenges of trading with confidence and achieve long-term success in the dynamic and competitive world of financial markets.

CHAPTER X

Trading Psychology and Discipline

Importance of Discipline in Forex Trading

The foundation of successful forex trading is discipline, which is essential for assisting traders in reaching their financial objectives and navigating the currency market's volatile and frequently unpredictable character. In forex trading, discipline is the capacity to stick to a planned trading schedule, obey predetermined guidelines and tactics, and regulate one's emotions when faced with volatility and unpredictability in the market. It is impossible to exaggerate the significance of discipline in forex trading since it is the cornerstone of long-term success and steady profits.

Discipline is crucial in forex trading because it prevents traders from making snap judgments and emotionally charged decisions that might result in losses. Factors such as market sentiment, geopolitical developments, and economic indicators can impact the highly volatile foreign exchange market. Without self-control, traders could give in to feelings of greed, fear, or panic, which would lead them to stray from their trading strategy and act irrationally. Traders can avoid emotional trading and make judgments based on reason and analysis rather than feelings by being disciplined and adhering to their set trading guidelines.

Discipline also encourages consistency in trading performance, which is necessary for sustained success in the foreign exchange market. The capacity to carry out trades by a predetermined strategy over an extended period, irrespective of market conditions or brief variations in performance, is known as consistency. To be consistent, one must be disciplined in adhering to trading guidelines, controlling emotions, and sticking to a trading plan, even in the face of hardship. When faced with obstacles or disappointments, traders who need more discipline may stray from their plan or give up entirely, leading to inconsistent trading results.

Additionally, discipline aids traders in avoiding psychological traps like confirmation bias, overconfidence, and revenge trading that can impair trading success. While revenge trading can push traders to chase losses and make rash actions to recover losses swiftly, overconfidence can lead traders to take unnecessary risks or overlook warning indications. Confirmation bias can impair judgment and cause traders to disregard evidence contradicting their prejudices or preconceived notions. Traders who practice discipline can identify and lessen these psychological biases, which helps them make logical and objective trading judgments.

Discipline enhances trading success and benefits traders' general well-being and mental health. It can help traders manage stress, lower anxiety, and prevent burnout. Trading can be a challenging and stressful business. If traders follow a planned trading plan and exercise emotional restraint, they can approach trading with confidence and peace of mind, knowing that they follow a tried-and-true technique and abide by their guidelines.

In conclusion, attaining continuous profitability and long-term success in forex trading requires excellent discipline. A trader can successfully negotiate the intricacies of the forex market by adhering to a disciplined trading plan, observing set guidelines and tactics, controlling their emotions, and managing risk. In addition to enhancing trading performance, discipline benefits traders' general health and well-being lowing them to reach their financial objectives and prosper in the fast-paced, cutthroat world of forex trading.

Overcoming Trading Psychology Pitfalls

A key component of financial market success is avoiding trading psychology traps. The term "trading psychology" describes the psychological and emotional aspects that affect traders' behavior and decision-making while trading. Long-term success in trading requires mastering the technical and fundamental parts of the game and comprehending and controlling trade psychology. Traders frequently deal with psychological issues like anxiety, greed, overconfidence, impatience, and emotional attachment to transactions, which can hurt their performance. It takes self-awareness, self-control, and the implementation of practical psychological techniques to avoid these traps.

Fear, which may take many forms, including fear of losing money, FOMO, and making mistakes, is one of the most frequent trading psychology traps. Fear can immobilize traders, making them hesitate or second-guess their choices and preventing them from carrying out their strategy when making transactions. To overcome anxiety, traders need to recognize that losses are an inevitable aspect of trading, gain confidence in their trading and risk management tactics, and concentrate on managing what they can control rather than worrying about outside forces.

Another psychological trap that can result in unreasonable risk-taking and irrational decision-making is greed. Traders driven by greed may chase profits, disregard red flags, and cling to lost positions to win them back. Traders must control their greed by sticking to their trading plan, setting reasonable profit targets, and avoiding getting too hooked on profitable deals. Traders can lessen the adverse effects of greed on their trading performance by engaging in disciplined trading and concentrating on steady, long-term earnings rather than chasing significant gains.

Overconfidence is a typical psychological trap that can cause traders to overestimate their skills and incur needless risks. Overconfident traders run the danger of making serious mistakes by failing to conduct adequate due diligence, overly leveraging their holdings, and ignoring risk management standards. To overcome overconfidence, traders need to have a continual improvement mindset, stay humble, and seek out education and feedback. To make more educated and logical trading decisions, traders should be aware of their limitations and maintain a realistic sense of reality.

Another psychological trap that can prevent traders from succeeding in the market is impatience, especially for those who get impatient with sluggish progress or anticipate quick results. Traders that need more patience could overtrade, enter deals too quickly, or close positions too soon, losing out on possible gains. To overcome their impatience, traders need to practice self-control and patience, stick to their trading plan, and fight the need to act on impulse. Traders can steer clear of snap judgments based on transient changes in the market by concentrating on long-term objectives and having faith in the process.

A psychological trap that can impair judgment and cause traders to hang onto losing positions longer than required is an emotional connection to trades. Even when it is evident that a deal is not going as intended, traders may get emotionally invested in it, waiting for it to turn around or refusing to accept a loss. Traders who want to overcome emotional attachment must learn to be objective and detached, recognize that losses are a necessary part of the trading process, and be prepared to cut their losses and move on when needed. Traders can enhance their overall performance and steer clear of sentiment-driven judgments by taking a logical and emotionless approach to trading.

In conclusion, success in the financial markets requires avoiding the traps of trading psychology. By understanding and regulating emotions, including fear, greed, overconfidence, impatience, and emotional attachment to transactions, traders may increase their overall performance, stick to their trading plan, and make better-informed and sensible decisions. Gaining self-awareness, self-control, and efficient psychological techniques are essential for avoiding trading psychology mistakes and becoming successful long-term traders.

Developing a Winning Mindset

One must cultivate a winning mindset to succeed in any pursuit, including trading in the financial markets. A winning mindset comprises various attitudes, convictions, and actions that empower traders to approach the market with self-assurance, grit, and self-control. It entails having a positive outlook, remaining mentally tough, and embracing a growth mentality that views obstacles as chances for development. Having a winning mentality is essential for conquering challenges, handling disappointments, enduring hardship, and attaining steady financial success in trading.

Keeping a positive view and attitude is one of the most important aspects of a winning mindset. When faced with obstacles and disappointments, traders can maintain their resolve, motivation, and focus by adopting a positive outlook. Traders with a winning mindset approach each trading day with optimism and enthusiasm, believing in their potential to succeed and achieve their goals rather than obsessing over past losses or mistakes. Traders can learn to be positive and productive despite adversity by practicing gratitude, positive affirmations, and visualization exercises.

Another crucial component of cultivating a winning mindset in trading is mental toughness. Mental toughness is the capacity to endure in the face of difficulty and to remain composed, focused, and composed under pressure. A winning mindset enables traders to regulate their emotions, preserve self-control, and adhere to their trading strategy despite market volatility and unpredictability. Trading can be an emotionally taxing endeavor. Resilience, self-control, and the capacity to overcome obstacles head-on are necessary for building mental toughness.

Developing a successful mindset in trading also requires adopting a growth mindset. The foundation of a growth mindset is the conviction that aptitude, effort, experience, and education can all be used to improve one's intelligence, skills, and abilities. Growth-minded traders look at obstacles as chances for personal development, ask for and welcome constructive criticism, and consider mistakes as important teaching moments rather than setbacks. Traders can break free from self-limiting ideas, step beyond their comfort zone, and continually change and adapt to shifting market conditions by embracing a growth mentality.

Another crucial component of cultivating a winning attitude in trading is establishing specific objectives and upholding a feeling of purpose. Setting and achieving goals helps traders stay motivated, focused, and dedicated to their trading endeavors. Whether hitting a particular profit threshold, perfecting a specific trading technique, or accomplishing a personal milestone, traders can maintain their discipline and motivation even in the face of adversity when they have well-defined goals. Traders can monitor their progress and recognize accomplishments by establishing attainable goals and decomposing them into smaller, more doable steps.

Moreover, keeping a winning mindset in trading requires building resilience. "resilience" describes the capacity to overcome obstacles, overcome setbacks, and flourish in the face of hardship. A winning mindset enables traders to remain resilient and composed despite setbacks or losses. Trading may be an exhilarating ride with ups and downs. Creating a support system, learning coping mechanisms, and continuing to be positive and have perspective amid hardship are all necessary for growing resilience.

To sum up, cultivating a winning mindset is crucial to succeeding in trading. A growth mentality, resilience building, mental toughness, goal-setting, and positivity-building are all components of a winning mindset. By cultivating these traits and behaviors, traders can approach trading with confidence, discipline, and endurance, which will help them overcome obstacles, deal with failures, and consistently make money in the financial markets. A winning mentality is essential for personal development and fulfillment in many facets of life and trading success.

Learning from Mistakes

One of the main advantages of learning from trading errors is gaining important insights into one's trading strategy and decision-making process. Every error committed gives traders insightful information about what went wrong and why, allowing them to pinpoint areas of weakness in their strategy and make the required corrections. Whether it's a lousy trade execution, a misguided analysis, or a lack of discipline, every error is a chance for introspection and self-evaluation, which helps traders improve their abilities and advance in their profession.

Additionally, learning from failures promotes the growth of mental toughness and resilience in traders—two traits necessary for successful trading. Losses and setbacks are a natural part of the trading journey and may be emotionally taxing experiences. Traders can overcome setbacks by viewing them as chances for learning rather than failures and can recover with newfound tenacity and resolve. Learning from failures helps traders become more resilient, emotionally intelligent, and capable of remaining calm and focused under pressure—all skills necessary for surviving market ups and downs.

Acknowledging errors also promotes a growth mentality, essential for ongoing development and sustained trading performance. Traders with a growth mentality see errors as opportunities for improvement rather than as things to avoid. They know that mistakes and setbacks are inevitable during the learning process and that trial and error is the road to mastery. Adopting a growth mentality makes traders more receptive to criticism, risk-takers, and robust against hardship, which helps them adjust to and prosper in the dynamic world of financial markets.

Learning from mistakes also aids in the improvement of traders' risk management abilities, which are critical for safeguarding capital and controlling downside risk. Inadequate risk management techniques, such as overleveraging, forgetting to set stop-loss orders, or neglecting risk-reward ratios, frequently cause trading errors. Traders can improve their risk management tactics and put in place more efficient protections to preserve their cash by examining their errors and spotting behavioral patterns that result in losses—learning from failures as a trader leads to a more disciplined approach to risk management over time, which is essential for sustained trading success.

Learning from mistakes boosts trading performance and increases traders' emotional intelligence and self-awareness, which helps them make better decisions and forge stronger bonds with others and themselves. By thinking back on their errors and comprehending the underlying causes, traders gain insights into their behavior, prejudices, and emotions. Because of their increased self-awareness, traders can better identify and control their feelings, make logical and impartial decisions, and cultivate positive connections.

In conclusion, a key component of trading success is learning from failures. By accepting failures as teaching opportunities, traders can improve their risk management techniques, cultivate a growth mindset, strengthen their resilience and mental fortitude, improve their self-awareness and emotional intelligence, and obtain important insights into their trading approach. Traders should treat errors as chances for learning and development rather than failures, understanding that each error they make moves them closer to their objectives and the success of trading.

Maintaining Consistency

Maintaining consistency is a hallmark of success in any endeavor, and trading in the financial markets is no exception. Consistency refers to the ability to execute trades according to a predefined strategy over time, regardless of market conditions or short-term fluctuations in performance. Consistency is essential for achieving long-term success in trading, as it allows traders to capitalize on their strengths, minimize their weaknesses, and build a track record of profitable trading over time.

Moreover, maintaining consistency in trading helps traders develop discipline and self-control, two essential qualities for success in the financial markets. Trading requires traders to adhere to a set of rules and principles, stick to their trading plan, and resist the temptation to deviate from their strategy based on short-term fluctuations in the market. Consistency in execution requires discipline, patience, and the ability to maintain emotional control, even during periods of uncertainty or volatility. Traders who maintain consistency in their approach to trading are better equipped to manage their emotions, avoid impulsive decisions, and stay focused on their long-term goals.

Consistency also contributes to developing good trading habits and routines essential for optimizing performance and productivity. Consistent routines help traders stay organized, disciplined, and focused on their trading activities, maximizing their efficiency and effectiveness in the markets. Whether conducting market analysis, executing trades, or reviewing performance metrics, consistent routines help traders establish a sense of rhythm and flow in their trading process, reducing stress and enhancing overall performance.

Furthermore, maintaining consistency in trading helps traders build a solid foundation of knowledge and experience over time. Consistent practice and repetition are crucial to mastering any skill, and trading is no exception. By consistently applying their trading strategy in various market conditions and learning from successes and failures, traders gain valuable insights into market dynamics, develop intuition and instinct, and refine their trading skills. Consistency in trading allows traders to build a repertoire of proven strategies and techniques, enabling them to adapt to changing market conditions and stay ahead of the curve.

In addition to improving trading performance, maintaining consistency helps traders build trust and credibility with others in the trading community. Consistent traders who demonstrate a track record of profitable trading over time are more likely to attract followers, investors, or partners who are drawn to their reliability and predictability. Consistency in trading builds reputation and credibility, opening doors to new opportunities for collaboration, partnership, or investment and enhancing the trader's standing in the trading community.

In conclusion, maintaining consistency is essential for achieving long-term success in trading. Consistency builds trust and credibility with oneself and others, fosters discipline and self-control, helps traders develop good trading habits and routines, contributes to accumulating knowledge and experience, and enhances reputation and credibility in the trading community. By maintaining consistency in their approach to trading, traders can maximize their chances of success and achieve their financial goals in the dynamic and competitive world of financial markets.

CHAPTER XI

Reviewing and Improving Your Performance

Keeping a Trading Journal

Keeping a trading log is an essential habit for traders who want to increase their performance, hone their techniques, and find sustained success in the financial markets. A trading log meticulously documents a trader's trading activity, including entries, exits, transaction justification, feelings, and observations. By keeping a thorough trading log, traders can improve their trading abilities and outcomes, which can help them recognize patterns, strengths, and flaws in their trading habits.

Additionally, maintaining a trading notebook fosters the development of emotional intelligence and self-awareness, which are critical for successful trading. Trading involves a lot of emotion, and traders who monitor their feelings and state of mind can better identify and control these aspects of their emotions. Traders can detect behavioral patterns or psychological biases that could impact their decision-making process by documenting their emotional state before, during, and after each trade. This self-awareness enables traders to make more logical and impartial trading decisions by identifying when they are feeling fear, greed, or other emotions that could impair their judgment.

A trading notebook not only keeps account of trade entries and exits but also gives traders a place to evaluate their performance, examine their errors, and pinpoint areas for development. Traders can examine previous trades, analyze trade results, and determine whether they successfully adhered to their trading plan and strategy using notebooks. Through a rigorous and objective analysis of their trades, traders can pinpoint common faults or errors, including overtrading, rash decisions, or disregard for risk management guidelines, and take appropriate action to rectify them. Through self-reflection and self-evaluation, traders can grow from their mistakes and improve their trading abilities and outcomes.

Moreover, a trading notebook is an invaluable educational resource that helps traders monitor their development and assess their performance over time. By meticulously recording their trading path, traders can evaluate their progress, commemorate their victories, and recognize their accomplishments. Keeping a trading journal helps traders keep motivated and focused on their long-term goals by assisting them to create reasonable goals and benchmarks for themselves and monitor their progress toward those goals. Even in difficult circumstances or downturns, traders can maintain discipline, accountability, and commitment to their trading plan by routinely reading their trading notebooks.

To sum up, maintaining a trading notebook is a crucial habit for traders hoping to raise their game and succeed in the long run in the financial markets. Traders can obtain critical insights into their trading behavior, recognize patterns, strengths, and weaknesses, and make well-informed decisions to improve their trading abilities and outcomes by keeping a thorough journal of their trading activity, feelings, and observations. On the path to trading mastery, a trading notebook may be a handy tool for self-awareness, self-reflection, and constant progress. It can also help traders stay motivated, focused, and disciplined.

Performance Analysis Techniques

Keeping a trading log is an essential habit for traders who want to increase their performance, hone their techniques, and find sustained success in the financial markets. A trader's trading activity, including entry, exits, transaction justification, feelings, and observations, is meticulously documented in a trading log. A trader can improve their trading abilities and outcomes by keeping a thorough trading log, which can help them recognize patterns, strengths, and flaws in their trading habit.

A thorough record of a trader's trading activities is one of the main advantages of maintaining a trading journal. By recording every transaction, traders may monitor their progress over time and examine their patterns and tendencies regarding entry and exit locations, position sizes, stop-loss levels, and profit targets. Traders can use this comprehensive record to determine the most successful trading techniques, the ideal markets or timeframes for their purposes, and the setups and conditions that result in positive transactions. Regular analysis of one's trading notebook can help traders identify their areas of strength and weakness and help them make the required corrections to improve.

Additionally, maintaining a trading notebook fosters the development of emotional intelligence and self-awareness, which are critical for successful trading. Trading involves a lot of emotion, and traders who monitor their feelings and state of mind can better identify and control these aspects of their feelings. Traders can detect behavioral patterns or psychological biases that could impact their decision-making process by documenting their emotional state before, during, and after each trade. This self-awareness enables traders to make more logical and impartial trading decisions by identifying when they are feeling fear, greed, or other emotions that could impair their judgment.

A trading notebook not only keeps account of trade entries and exits but also gives traders a place to evaluate their performance, examine their errors, and pinpoint areas for development. Traders can examine previous trades, analyze trade results, and determine whether they successfully adhered to their trading plan and strategy using notebooks. Through a rigorous and objective analysis of their trades, traders can pinpoint common faults or errors, including overtrading, rash decisions, or disregard for risk management guidelines, and take appropriate action to rectify them. Through self-reflection and self-evaluation, traders can grow from their mistakes and improve their trading abilities and outcomes.

Moreover, a trading notebook is an invaluable educational resource that helps traders monitor their development and assess their performance over time. By meticulously recording their trading path, traders can evaluate their progress, commemorate their victories, and recognize their accomplishments. Keeping a trading journal helps traders keep motivated and focused on their long-term goals by assisting them to create reasonable goals and benchmarks for themselves and monitor their progress toward those goals. Even in difficult circumstances or downturns, traders can maintain discipline, accountability, and commitment to their trading plan by routinely reading their trading notebooks.

To sum up, maintaining a trading notebook is a crucial habit for traders hoping to raise their game and succeed in the long run in the financial markets. Traders can obtain critical insights into their trading behavior, recognize patterns, strengths, and weaknesses, and make well-informed decisions to improve their trading abilities and outcomes by keeping a thorough journal of their trading activity, feelings, and observations. On the path to trading mastery, a trading notebook may be a handy tool for self-awareness, self-reflection, and constant progress. It can also help traders stay motivated, focused, and disciplined.

Identifying Strengths and Weaknesses

A trader's path to steady success in the financial markets begins with assessing their strengths and shortcomings. Knowing where they stand firm and where they need to grow, traders leverage their strengths and address areas that may be impeding their performance. Through a comprehensive self-evaluation and analysis of their trading behavior, methods, and results, traders can learn much about what makes them unique and what needs improvement.

Objectively evaluating one's trading performance is one of the first stages of determining strengths and flaws. This entails looking into performance metrics, including win rate, average profit/loss per trade, maximum drawdown, risk-adjusted return measurements, and assessing trade outcomes and prior trade analysis. Traders can more precisely evaluate their strengths and weaknesses by looking back at their trading history to find areas of concern and patterns of success.

Traders should also evaluate their methods and trading strategies to see what is effective and needs improvement. This includes assessing how well their trade management strategies, risk management procedures, and entrance and exit requirements work. Traders must contemplate whether their chosen approach aligns with their preferred trading approach, level of risk tolerance, financial objectives, and ability to adjust to varying market circumstances. Traders can improve their overall performance by pinpointing areas for optimization and improvement by critically evaluating their trading approach.

Additionally, traders must consider the psychological and emotional aspects of themselves that might influence their trading choices. Fear, greed, and overconfidence are just a few examples of emotions that can impair judgment and cause impulsive or unreasonable trading activity.

Traders can create techniques to better control their feelings by looking at how they feel while they trade and detecting any trends or triggers that might affect their actions. This could be engaging in mindfulness exercises, scheduling time for introspection, or asking a mentor or trading coach for help.

Additionally, traders must think about their assets and liabilities that do not directly relate to trading and could affect how well they do in the markets. For instance, someone with a background in economics or finance might comprehend market fundamentals more deeply, and someone with excellent analytical abilities might be better at technical analysis. On the other hand, traders who need more self-control or time management abilities could find it challenging to stick to a consistent trading strategy. Traders can become more well-rounded by leveraging their skills and improving their areas of weakness by identifying their strengths and limitations in different places.

The following stage for traders is to create a plan to capitalize on their strengths and solve their deficiencies after determining their strengths and limitations. This could entail honing their trading approach, enforcing more stringent risk control procedures, or emphasizing the development of their emotional grit and self-control. To monitor their performance and hold themselves responsible, traders should develop SMART (specific, measurable, attainable, relevant, and time-bound) goals for themselves. With consistent examination and modification of their trading plan in response to constant performance monitoring, traders can enhance their abilities over time.

In conclusion, one of the most critical steps a trader can take to become a consistent winner in the financial markets is to assess their strengths and shortcomings. Through a comprehensive self-evaluation and analysis of their trading behavior, methods, and results, traders can learn a great deal about what makes them unique and what needs improvement. In the fast-paced and cutthroat world of trading, traders can improve their overall performance and reach their financial objectives by using their strengths and enhancing their shortcomings via ongoing learning and development.

Continuous Learning and Adaptation

Success in the dynamic and always-shifting world of the financial markets largely depends on one's ability to learn and adapt constantly. In a world where trends, technologies, and market circumstances are ever-changing, traders must commit to lifelong learning and adaptability to stay profitable and competitive. Continuous learning entails keeping up with market trends, picking up new methods, and honing already acquired abilities. On the other hand, adaptation calls for the capacity to modify trading tactics and approaches in reaction to shifting market conditions.

Continuous learning helps traders stay ahead of the curve and adjust to changing market conditions more skillfully, which is one of its main advantages. By keeping up with industry advancements, geopolitical events, and macroeconomic trends, traders can predict future market movements and modify their strategy accordingly. Additionally, traders can broaden their toolbox and more effectively adjust to shifting market conditions by learning new trading strategies and tools. For instance, becoming knowledgeable about technical analysis indicators or algorithmic trading strategies can assist traders in seeing fresh possibilities and enhancing their ability to make decisions in quickly shifting markets.

Additionally, ongoing education promotes a growth attitude, which is necessary for trading success over the long run. The idea that intelligence, aptitude, and skills can be acquired via work, experience, and education defines a growth mindset. A growth attitude in trading makes a trader more receptive to criticism, risk-taking, and resilient to losses. By accepting obstacles as chances for development and recognizing setbacks as priceless teaching moments, traders can enhance their abilities over time and adjust to shifting market conditions brighter.

Continuous learning also aids dealers in maintaining their competitiveness in a crowded and cutthroat industry. To keep ahead of the competition, traders need to make the most of the easy access to information and educational tools the digital era offers. Continuous learning enables traders to remain current on the newest trading techniques, market trends, and technological developments through various activities, including reading trading books, watching webinars, and engaging in online forums and communities. Traders can obtain a competitive advantage and set themselves up for market success by continuing to be proactive and involved in their education.

Adaptability is just as important as ongoing education to navigate the volatile and constantly shifting financial markets. Due to various reasons, including economic data releases, geopolitical events, and shifts in investor attitude, market conditions can change quickly. As a result, traders need to be prepared to modify their strategy as necessary. They are being adaptable means being nimble, agile, and sensitive to shifts in the market dynamics. It also means having the courage to try new things, make mistakes, and refine trade plans in response to feedback and market conditions as they arise.

Additionally, traders must be systematic and impartial in their decision-making to adapt. Although it may be alluring to adhere to a strict trading plan or strategy, traders need to be prepared to modify their tactics in light of fresh knowledge and changes in the market. This could be minimizing losses as soon as possible, reducing risk exposure when things are unclear, or seizing fresh chances as they present themselves. Traders can increase earnings, reduce losses, and better take advantage of shifting market trends by maintaining discipline and flexibility.

To sum up, the keys to success in trading are constant learning and adaptability. Traders can remain ahead of the curve and spot fresh profit chances by dedicating themselves to lifelong learning and keeping up with market trends. Additionally, traders can maximize their chances of success by adjusting their plans and methods by being adaptable, agile, and quick to changes in market conditions. Not only are constant learning and adaptation essential for surviving in today's competitive and fast-paced market climate, but they are also necessary for traders to prosper and achieve long-term success.

CHAPTER XII

Expanding Your Forex Trading Knowledge

Advanced Technical Analysis Tools

Advanced technical analysis tools are essential resources for traders who want to learn more about market trends, patterns, and possible price moves. These tools provide a more sophisticated and nuanced approach to studying price movement and making trading decisions, while simple tools like trendlines, moving averages, and support and resistance levels offer useful information about market dynamics.

Fibonacci retracement is one of the sophisticated technical analysis strategies that traders employ frequently. This tool, which is based on important Fibonacci ratios, is derived from the Fibonacci sequence and aids in identifying possible levels of support and resistance. Fibonacci retracement levels are used by traders to predict probable price reversals or continuation patterns, which aids in the identification of the best times to enter and exit trades. By utilizing Fibonacci retracement in their analysis, traders can uncover high-probability trading opportunities and improve their grasp of market movements.

Furthermore, traders frequently use sophisticated chart patterns—like Elliott Wave theory and harmonic patterns—to assess market trends and project future price moves. Based on geometric ratios and symmetry in price action, traders can spot possible reversal or continuation patterns with harmonic patterns like the Gartley and Butterfly patterns. Contrarily, Elliott Wave theory asserts that market trends develop in recurring wave patterns, which enables traders to predict future price movements using wave counts and wave structures. Traders can enhance their comprehension of market dynamics and forecast future price movements by becoming proficient in complex chart patterns.

Moreover, momentum indicators like the Stochastic Oscillator and Moving Average Convergence Divergence (MACD) are examples of advanced technical analysis tools. These indicators assist traders in determining possible trend reversals, determining the intensity and direction of market trends, and producing buy or sell signals. The Stochastic Oscillator compares the market's closing price today to the range of prices over a given period. In contrast, the MACD calculates the convergence and divergence of two moving averages. Traders can better manage risk, validate trends, and pinpoint entry and exit points by integrating momentum indicators into their analysis.

Advanced technical analysis tools frequently include custom indicators and algorithms created by traders or quantitative analysts to obtain a competitive edge in the markets. These custom indicators may use sophisticated mathematical models, artificial intelligence, or machine learning to evaluate market data and spot trading opportunities. Custom indicators provide traders with additional insights into price fluctuations and market trends, enhancing their current research. Traders can improve their trading performance and gain a competitive advantage using sophisticated technical analysis tools.

To sum up, sophisticated technical analysis tools are essential for providing traders with a greater understanding of market trends, patterns, and possible price moves. With tools like Fibonacci retracement, relative strength index, advanced chart patterns, and custom indicators, traders may analyze price action and make trading decisions with a comprehensive and nuanced approach. By learning how to use sophisticated technical analysis tools, traders can become more adept at spotting high-probability trading opportunities, controlling risk, and achieving steady success in the cutthroat world of financial markets.

In-depth Fundamental Analysis Techniques

For traders and investors looking to comprehend the intrinsic value of financial assets and make wise judgments in the markets, in-depth fundamental research techniques are indispensable. Fundamental research goes deeper into the underlying variables influencing asset prices, such as macroeconomic trends, corporate financial performance, and economic indicators. In contrast, technical analysis concentrates on price movement and market trends. Traders can uncover opportunities and hazards, understand the underlying worth of assets, and make better investment decisions by performing in-depth fundamental analysis.

Economic analysis is an essential analysis technique that traders employ extensively. It entails examining economic indicators and data to evaluate an economy's state and future prospects. To assess an economy's general health and trajectory, traders closely monitor critical economic indicators such as GDP, employment statistics, inflation rates, and trends in consumer spending. Traders can predict future shifts in market sentiment, spot new trends, and modify their investing strategy by examining economic data and trends.

Furthermore, fundamental analysis examines corporate financial statements and performance indicators to evaluate certain businesses' economic standing and prospects. To assess a company's revenue, profitability, debt levels, and cash flow creation, traders review financial statements such as income statements, balance sheets, and cash flow statements. To evaluate a company's valuation and growth prospects, traders often examine performance indicators, including return on equity (ROE), price-to-earnings (P/E) ratios, and earnings per share (EPS). Traders can find cheap or expensive stocks, weigh the benefits and drawbacks of investing in a specific firm, and make better investment decisions by performing in-depth financial analysis.

Moreover, industry analysis is one of the fundamental approaches that examine the larger industry dynamics and trends that might affect the performance of specific businesses within a sector. Traders evaluate competitive positioning, market share, technical innovation, regulatory environment, and industry strength to determine whether industries offer excellent investment opportunities and great growth prospects. By examining industry trends and dynamics, traders can spot new trends, predict changes in the market, and arrange their portfolios to take advantage of openings.

Furthermore, macroeconomic patterns and geopolitical variables that could affect asset values and financial markets are examined in fundamental research. To analyze market mood and identify potential dangers and opportunities, traders evaluate global economic trends, geopolitical tensions, interest rates, and central bank policies. Traders can better control risk by anticipating future market moves and modifying their investing strategy to macroeconomic trends and geopolitical developments.

Furthermore, qualitative analysis—which evaluates qualitative elements including brand reputation, corporate governance procedures, management quality, and competitive advantages—is frequently incorporated into fundamental analysis approaches. Traders analyze a company's long-term prospects and competitive position by considering corporate culture, strategic vision, and management's past performance. Traders can evaluate a company's capacity to execute its strategy, learn much about the management team, and make better investment selections using qualitative analysis.

In summary, traders and investors who want to comprehend the inherent value of financial assets and make wise market judgments must have access to comprehensive fundamental research techniques. Traders can make better investment decisions by gaining important insights into market dynamics, identifying potential opportunities and hazards, and assessing macroeconomic factors, industry trends, business financial performance, and qualitative aspects. Even though fundamental analysis necessitates a deep comprehension of financial and economic principles, becoming proficient in these methods can give traders a competitive advantage in the fast-paced and cutthroat world of financial markets.

Exploring Alternative Trading Instruments

Traders should investigate alternative trading instruments to diversify their holdings, protect themselves from danger, and take advantage of new opportunities in the financial markets. Alternative trading instruments have special benefits and features that can supplement or improve conventional investment techniques, even if standard trading instruments like stocks, bonds, and currencies are still widely used by investors.

Cryptocurrencies are an alternate trading tool that is becoming increasingly well-liked among traders. Bitcoin, Ethereum, and Ripple are examples of cryptocurrencies that have arisen as a new asset class with enormous growth and innovation potential. Cryptocurrencies are decentralized digital assets built on blockchain technology and offer advantages like efficiency, security, and transparency. They differ from traditional currencies. Through exchanges or derivative products like futures and options, traders can make predictions about the movements in the price of cryptocurrencies, which can help them diversify their holdings and increase their returns.

Commodities, which comprise assets like precious metals, agricultural products, energy resources, and industrial metals, are another type of alternative trading tool; in addition to providing diversification advantages, commodities hedge against inflation and geopolitical concerns. Through exchange-traded funds (ETFs) or futures contracts, traders can invest directly in commodities, giving them exposure to actual assets and the opportunity to profit from changes in commodity market prices. Furthermore, commodities are desirable for portfolio diversification because they frequently correlate little with traditional asset classes.

Derivatives like options, futures, and swaps are also considered alternative trading instruments since they offer traders various flexible options for hedging against risks, making predictions about market movements, and making money. Using leverage and hedging tactics, derivatives enable traders to increase returns, leverage their capital, and better control risk. Derivatives give traders more flexibility and liquidity in their trading activities by exposing them to various asset classes, such as equities, bonds, currencies, and commodities, without actually holding the underlying assets.

In addition, alternative trading instruments include assets like venture capital, real estate, hedge funds, and private equity, which present particular chances for alpha production and diversification. These investments protect against loss and increase total portfolio returns because they often correlate little with traditional asset types. By investing in alternative assets directly or through specialist funds and vehicles, traders can access unique markets and methods that might not be accessible through standard investment channels.

Thematic investments like environmental, social, and governance (ESG) funds, impact investing, and socially responsible investing (SRI), which seek to provide favorable social and ecological outcomes in addition to financial returns, are also included in the category of alternative trading instruments. Traders may promote sustainable practices and benefit the environment and society by investing in businesses and initiatives that share their values. Traders could make competitive profits by aligning their investments with their values through these investments.

In conclusion, traders can now take advantage of fresh chances to diversify their holdings, manage risk, and profit from new developments in the financial markets by investigating different trading instruments. Traders looking to broaden their trading horizons can access many possibilities, from commodities and cryptocurrencies to derivatives, alternative investments, and thematic investments. In the fast-paced, constantly evolving world of finance, traders can increase portfolio diversification, boost risk-adjusted returns, and accomplish their financial objectives by implementing alternative trading instruments into their investing strategy.

Introduction to Algorithmic Trading

The advent of algorithmic trading represents a significant advancement in the functioning of financial markets. Algorithmic trading, often known as automated trading or black-box trading, uses computer algorithms to execute trading orders automatically based on established criteria and rules. This trading strategy has gained popularity in recent years due to its ability to execute trades quickly, precisely, and efficiently while eliminating human emotions' impact on trading decisions.

One of the primary benefits of algorithmic trading is its ability to execute trades at fast speeds, significantly exceeding the capabilities of human traders. Algorithmic trading systems use powerful computer algorithms and high-speed data networks to evaluate market circumstances, find trading opportunities, and execute deals in milliseconds. This enables traders to seize ephemeral market opportunities and respond to changing market conditions quickly and efficiently.

Furthermore, algorithmic trading allows for greater precision and accuracy in trade execution than human trading. Algorithms can be built to execute trades based on specific factors such as price, quantity, and timing, ensuring that deals are done at ideal levels. Furthermore, algorithmic trading systems can evaluate massive volumes of market data and information, find patterns and trends, and make trading decisions based on objective criteria unaffected by human emotions or prejudices.

Furthermore, algorithmic trading can help traders control risk more effectively by using sophisticated risk management approaches and tactics. Algorithms can be developed to monitor market situations in real-time, alter trading parameters dynamically, and incorporate risk controls to prevent losses. This limits traders' exposure to market volatility and unexpected events while improving their risk-adjusted profits.

Furthermore, algorithmic trading allows traders to back test and optimize their trading techniques more effectively. Simulating trading techniques against historical market data will enable traders to examine their strategies' performance and viability, discover any weaknesses or defects, and make required improvements before deploying them in live markets. This enables traders to fine-tune their methods, maximize their performance, and increase their chances of success in the market.

Furthermore, algorithmic trading offers dealers greater flexibility and scalability in their trading operations. Automated trading systems can be set up to trade numerous markets, asset classes, and trading venues simultaneously, allowing traders to diversify their trading tactics and capitalize on opportunities in various market situations. Furthermore, algorithmic trading systems can easily handle high quantities of deals, allowing dealers to expand their trading operations without requiring new human resources or equipment.

Finally, the introduction of algorithmic trading marks a big step forward in the operation of financial markets. Algorithmic trading systems use complex computer algorithms and high-speed data networks to execute deals quickly, precisely, and efficiently while decreasing human emotions' impact on trading decisions. Algorithmic trading provides traders with increased speed, precision, accuracy, risk management capabilities, back testing and optimization tools, flexibility, and scalability in their trading operations. As technology advances, algorithmic trading is expected to become increasingly essential in defining the future of financial markets.

Global Economic Trends and Their Impact on Forex

Global economic trends significantly impact the foreign exchange (forex) market, influencing currency valuations, exchange rates, and trading possibilities worldwide. The world's largest and most liquid financial market is the FX market, which is susceptible to changes in economic conditions, policies, and emotions across countries and regions. Forex traders and investors pay close attention to global economic trends because they provide valuable insights into prospective currency fluctuations, market volatility, and trading methods.

Economic growth and recession cycles are among the most important global economic trends influencing the FX market. Strong economic growth often causes a country's currency to appreciate as investors seek higher returns and new investment opportunities. On the other hand, economic recessions or slowdowns can cause a currency to fall in value as investors migrate to safe-haven assets and lower-risk investments. Forex traders monitor economic growth indicators such as GDP growth rates, employment data, and consumer spending patterns to analyze the strength and prospects of various economies and forecast probable currency movements.

Central banks, with their monetary policy actions and interest rate differentials, play a pivotal role in influencing FX market movements. They determine interest rates and adopt monetary policies to achieve a variety of economic goals, including controlling inflation, boosting economic growth, and ensuring financial stability. Changes in interest rates or monetary policy outlooks can cause revisions in currency valuations and exchange rates as investors modify their expectations and portfolio allocations. By closely monitoring central bank announcements, interest rate decisions, and policymaker pronouncements, forex traders can forecast prospective monetary policy changes and their influence on currency valuations.

Geopolitical events and developments can cause significant volatility and uncertainty in forex markets, directly affecting currency valuations and exchange rates. Political instability, conflicts, trade difficulties, and diplomatic relations between countries can all cause fluctuations in investor sentiment and risk perceptions, influencing currency demand and market dynamics.

Elections, referendums, geopolitical crises, and trade talks are examples of geopolitical events that can cause sharp and significant fluctuations in currency prices as traders review geopolitical risks and their consequences for economic stability and growth.

Furthermore, trade dynamics and global trade imbalances can influence forex markets and currency valuations. Changes in international trade policy, tariffs, and trade agreements can all impact trade flows, currency demand, and exchange rates. Trade surpluses and deficits can cause a country's currency to appreciate or depreciate as investors assess trade imbalances and their possible impact on economic performance and stability. Forex traders carefully monitor trade data, negotiations, and other trade-related developments to anticipate prospective currency moves and trading opportunities.

Finally, global economic trends shape the dynamics of the forex market by influencing currency valuations, exchange rates, and trading opportunities worldwide. Economic growth and recession cycles, monetary policy decisions, geopolitical events, and trade dynamics are some significant elements that influence currency market movements and trading techniques. Forex traders must diligently watch global economic trends, understand their possible impact on currency markets, and modify their trading techniques to traverse the dynamic and interrelated world of forex trading successfully.

CONCLUSION

In conclusion, " Mastering Forex Trading: Strategies for Success in the Global Currency Market: A Comprehensive Guide to Unlocking Financial Freedom" is an indispensable resource for traders seeking to navigate the complexities of the forex market and achieve their financial goals. Throughout the book, readers have comprehensive insights, practical strategies, and valuable techniques to enhance their trading skills and unlock financial freedom.

This book provides readers with a holistic understanding of forex trading by delving into fundamental and technical analysis, risk management strategies, trading psychology, and advanced trading techniques. It empowers them to make informed decisions in the dynamic global currency market.

Moreover, "Mastering Forex Trading" goes beyond theory by offering real-world examples, case studies, and practical tips that enable traders to apply their newfound knowledge effectively. Whether readers are beginners looking to establish a solid foundation in forex trading or seasoned traders seeking to refine their strategies, this book caters to traders of all levels and aspirations.

Ultimately, "Mastering Forex Trading" equips readers with the tools, confidence, and expertise needed to thrive in the competitive world of forex trading, paving the way for success and financial independence.

Thank you for buying and reading/ listening to our book. If you found this book useful/ helpful please take a few minutes and leave a review on the platform where you purchased our book. Your feedback matters greatly to us.

9 798330 209156